Do You Believe in Magic?

Most of us believe that magic is just an illusion, not something to really believe in. We attempt to rationalize our lives because our Western way of thinking tells us that if we can't see it, taste it, smell it, touch it, or hear it, then it (that illusive entity) must not exist. The term magic conjures up the illusion of an unreal fantasy world. This illusion is usually left to languish in a dormant part of our psyche. Our minds drift to this place in our consciousness from time to time, when life gets too tough to bear, and stress is uncontrollable. We retreat to this place for respite, but never really expect to live our fantasies. That, of course, is for other people—the special, gifted, lucky few. It is time to dispel this myth and accept the fact that what we dream about in our most private moments can actually be our reality.

Just what does it mean to live a magical life? I'll explain. According to *Webster's New Collegiate Dictionary*, magic is "an extraordinary power or influence from a supernatural source." The "supernatural source" and "extraordinary power" simultaneously exist within each of us. It is our spiritual destiny to acknowledge and employ them, to live life to the fullest. To live magically then, would be to live a life that is shaped and greatly affected by our enchanted supernatural power. This is a perfectly natural way for us to live because we, by our birthright, are born embodying this divine power. We are therefore divine magicians, empowered by and skilled in the art of sacred magic.

—*Adrian Calabrese*

About the Author

Adrian Calabrese, Ph.D., Msc.D., ClH., holds a doctorate in Psychical Research, another in Metaphysics, and is a certified clinical hypnotherapist. A psychic, channel, medium, psychic artist, holistic practitioner, inspirational speaker, and minister, she has worked extensively with intuitive and pastoral counseling, past life regression, and spiritual energy healing, and is the founder and director of the Metaphysical Center for Arts & Sciences and pastor of the Metaphysical Church of the Spirit. Her other talents include backgrounds in performance, art, and broadcasting.

To Write to the Author

If you wish to contact the author or would like more information about this book, please write to the author in care of Llewellyn Worldwide and we will forward your request. Both the author and publisher appreciate hearing from you and learning of your enjoyment of this book and how it has helped you. Llewellyn Worldwide cannot guarantee that every letter written to the author can be answered, but all will be forwarded. Write to:

Adrian Calabrese
C/o Llewellyn Worldwide
P.O. Box 64383, Dept. 0-7387-0311-7
St. Paul, MN 55164-0383, U.S.A.

Please enclose a self-addressed stamped envelope for reply, or $1.00 to cover costs. If outside U.S.A., enclose international postal reply coupon.

Many of Llewellyn's authors have websites with additional information and resources. For more information, please visit our website at http://www.llewellyn.com.

10 Spiritual Steps to a Magical Life

Meditations & Affirmations for Personal Growth & Happiness

Adrian Calabrese, Ph.D.

2003
Llewellyn Publications
St. Paul, Minnesota 55164-0383, U.S.A.

FIRST EDITION
First Printing, 2003

Book interior design and editing by Connie Hill
Cover design by Kevin R. Brown
Cover image © 2002 by Photodisc

Library of Congress Cataloging-in-Publication Data
Calabrese, Adrian
10 spiritual steps to a magical life : meditations & affirmations
for personal growth & happiness / Adrian Calabrese.
p. cm.
Includes bibliographical references and index.
ISBN 0-7387-0311-7
1. Magic. 2. Spiritual life—Miscellanea.
I. Title: Ten spiritual steps to a magical life. II. Title
BF1611.C34   2003   133.4'3—dc21   2002027453

Llewellyn Publications
A Division of Llewellyn Worldwide, Ltd.
P.O. Box 64383, Dept. 0-7387-0311-7
St. Paul, MN 55164-0383, U.S.A.
www.llewellyn.com

Printed in the United States of America

Dedicated, with love, to
Lynn Heuermann,
my soul sister, my friend,
whose faith in this book, and its author,
is beyond belief.

Also by Adrian Calabrese

*How to Get Everything You Ever Wanted: Complete Guide
to Using Your Psychic Common Sense,* 2000

Also available in Spanish:
Obtenga éxito: Utilice el poder de su mente, 2002

Table of Contents

Acknowledgments

I believe that we are, we live, we succeed, because we have all been divinely blessed, therefore my thanks must first be to God, the infinite Creator, who guides our every thought, deed, and word, and who really wrote this book. I thank, too, all the loving energies in spirit, angelic and otherwise, who continue to guide my work.

My thanks goes next to my parents, Ann and Rudy Calabrese, for their constant, loving support, and to my family, dear friends (you know who you are), and loyal church members.

I am most grateful to the spirit clan at Llewellyn, who felt I had something valuable to say, and made it possible for me to say it. My special thanks goes to Nancy Mostad for the steady support and encouragement she so generously gave to this book, to Connie Hill for her wise and expert edit, and to Lisa Novak and Kevin R. Brown for the beautiful cover.

In closing, I bless and thank all the souls whose stories appear in this book, and you, dear readers, for the courage to seek wisdom, guidance, and joy as you travel along your path to your magical life.

Blessings on your journey!

I painfully remember a time when I was searching to fill an inexplicable void in my life. Try as I might, I just couldn't figure out what was missing, and why, no matter how successful I was, that nagging feeling of emptiness pervaded my every waking moment.

Churches, religions, and self-help groups didn't work for me. Continuing my arduous search, I was divinely led to the philosophy of metaphysics, became an ordained minister, and subsequently met hundreds of people who shared my dilemma. There is an ache within all of us to express ourselves and to, as Henry David Thoreau said, "Go confidently in the direction of your dreams . . . live the life you have imagined."

It is obvious to me, now and in the last few years leading to the millennium, that there exists in our society a growing desire for a spiritual approach to life. Metaphysical books, such as *The Celestine Prophecy* by James Redfield, and *Conversations With God* by Neale Donald Walsch, are selling like hot cakes, and even made bestseller lists. It appears that many of us are eager to find answers to our questions, and are willing to do what it takes to get them. Intuitively, we know there is a way to live spiritually, in a harmony of mind, body, and soul—yet it seems elusive. I decided to write this book for the millions of us who want answers, but are disillusioned with the limiting rhetoric of traditional religion.

Combining spiritual principles with my own personal plan of action, I finally found a way to live a happy life, directly in touch with the power of my Spirit. I continue to live magically each day, as do many others who have followed my system, and you can, too.

In this book I outline a simple approach to living that exceeds any religious dogma, and offers you the opportunity for unlimited spiritual growth, far beyond that of any one tradition. I have attempted within these pages to give my readers the tools for creating a sacred, joyful, and abundant life that have worked so well for me. By tapping into our extraordinary divine power, anyone, from novice to advanced seeker, can benefit from developing these practical skills. The tools for creating and living a magical life are ready and waiting for us, woven by a benevolent Spirit into the very fabric of our minds, bodies, and souls.

I have organized this book into ten simple and clearly understandable steps for the newest spiritual seeker as well as the advanced student. Each step will guide you from the earliest stages of your spiritual work to the achievement of a comfortable balance of mind, body, and Spirit as a way of life. They will teach you to create a magical state of mind for yourself that will attract the right teachers, mentors, and fellow journeymen along your path. If you follow the steps faithfully, you will begin to see your life changing in a very special way. You will finally understand what it means to be in direct communication with God. Yes, God. Not only will you become happier and more sensitive to others, you will notice that suddenly you are attracting whatever your heart desires as well. This is a great byproduct of living magically—you get to have everything you want!

In addition to the ten magical steps, I have included a reflection or meditation exercise to get you thinking about your life and the changes that need to be made, in order for you to make magic happen. Each chapter ends with an affirmation or declarative statement of prayer that announces to God/Universe/Spirit that you are grabbing the gusto and going for the big prize in the contest of life—joy! These reflections and affirmations have worked for me and my clients and students, and I know they will work for you.

In my research and counseling work, I have found that those of us seeking the spiritual path are dissatisfied with the directives of the past. We are no longer blindly accepting what others dole out as truth. Instead, modern mystics want to discover the answers for themselves. We proponents of this way of thinking are setting forth on individual spiritual quests to find answers to the most intimate questions of our souls, and to truly form a living, active relationship with our Creator. In our quest we seek spiritual guidelines for life that do not hold to any traditional dogma, but, rather, open the Spirit to unlimited growth, far surpassing the dictates of any theory or viewpoint.

Your inner, or Spirit-Power, as I call it, can and will change the way you live when you commit to taking the first step on your spiritual path. You only need to acknowledge and welcome it and it will provide answers where there is confusion; guide you to a life of peace, love, and harmony with your world; and lead you to an existence that truly honors your Spirit.

We need only depend upon our own spiritual determination to live a magical life. It is time now for you to take the first step, and recognize that you hold within you a power that is so great and expansive that it is capable of unlimited achievement. This power is not a product of our learned or ingrained notions. It is the very essence of *who* you are. It can't be lost or diminished in any way. It is beyond all thought, philosophy, and religion. It is beyond belief.

Abracadabra! Welcome to the twenty-first century. You're thinking, "I barely made it through the end of the twentieth. What now? What happened to the 90s?" It seems almost as if a mystical sorcerer has waved his or her magic wand and we have been catapulted, unwittingly, into a new millennium. Some of us are looking forward to our futures with great anticipation, and others are confused and frustrated at the prospect. What is expected of us in this time of great change? More importantly, what do we expect of ourselves?

At this exciting time in human history, each of us needs to take an objective look at our life. Many of us are satisfied with the status quo, even if it means that our lives are dull, boring, and unfulfilled, not to mention devoid of joy. We may plod through our days without a clue as to how to get out of our rut, instinctively feeling that there must be something more, but we don't quite know what that something is.

Step 1

Accept Your Power

Believe and accept that you have the power to change your life

To change our lives and make the most of every minute we have on this planet, we might start by asking ourselves a few questions, and facing up to our answers: "Am I happy?" "Do I sense a spiritual connection to all of life?" "Can I honestly say that I am a person who feels ful- filled and satisfied?" "Are all the meaningful relation- ships of my life well balanced and joyful?" "Am I pros- perous and abundant?" If your answer to any of these questions is "no," then read on. Even if you think your life is on track, keep reading, because if your life really is in flow, you should never stop exploring new ways of thinking.

Of all the questions we might ask ourselves as we search our souls for the meaning of life, I suggest that there is one that we may not have considered. If you have chosen to read this book, chances are you have been attracted by the prospect of living beyond your present state of reality, having, doing, and being something more. If so, then this is the one question you must ask yourself, if you sincerely want to create an outstanding, exciting existence: "Am I living a truly magical life?"

Do You Believe In Magic?

Most of us believe that magic is just an illusion, not something to really believe in. We attempt to rationalize our lives because our Western way of thinking tells us that if we can't see it, taste it, smell it, touch it, or hear it, then it (that illusive entity) must not exist. The term "magic" conjures up the illusion of an unreal fantasy world. This illusion is usually left to languish in a dor- mant part of our psyche. Our minds drift to this place in our consciousness from time to time, when life gets too tough to bear and stress is uncontrollable. We retreat to this place for respite, but never really expect to live our fantasies. That, of course, is for other people—the special, gifted, lucky few. It is time to dispel this myth and accept the fact that what we dream about in our most private moments can actually be our reality.

Just what does it mean to live a magical life? According to *Webster's New Collegiate Dictionary*, a definition for the word "magic" is ". . . an extraordinary power or influence seemingly from a supernatural source." The supernatural source and extraordinary power simultaneously exist within each of us. It is our spiritual destiny to acknowledge and employ them to live life to the fullest. To live magically, then, would be to live a life that is shaped and greatly affected by our enchanted supernatural power. This is a perfectly natural way for us to live because we, by our birthright, are born embodying this divine power. We are, therefore, divine magicians, empowered by and skilled in the art of sacred magic.

You are living a magical life when you wake up each morning excited about the day. You are living magically if you are easily amazed at how well things go for you in your day-to-day dealings, and you are appreciated for the efforts you make. Sacred magic guides your life if your relationships with others are fun, interesting, peaceful, and loving. You are living a magical life if you are successful, if you are doing a job you love and are making a decent living at it. Magic is part of your life if all your earthly needs are met, if you easily draw and attract the people, events, and things you want and need into your life by merely desiring them. And finally, you are living magically if you feel a direct connection to the Source that created you and you have an ongoing, comfortable relationship with It. A sacred magician knows in his or her heart-of-hearts that he or she is never alone, and is always loved and treasured by his or her Creator. Magicians find tremendous joy in helping other people, animals, and the planet. When you see life as an adventure full of wonder and perceive struggle and pain as part of the process, challenges to be met and overcome, you are living a magical life.

Disney World, Here You Come!

I asked my friend Jeff to describe his idea of a magical life. His response was that he hoped it would be like living in Disney World, everyone and everything happy, sunny, bright, and cheery. His thoughts are of an enchanted world where anything is possible, your imagination can run free, and you get everything you ever wanted.

I've got news for Jeff, and for you. That world does exist, now, and you have direct access to it. I am not talking about taking a plane to Orlando, Florida, to see Mickey Mouse. I'm talking about learning to tap into the power you already have within you to change your life for the better. When you accept that your Spirit is much more powerful than your body, and that your world can take the shape you want it to, you, too, can live in a magic kingdom everyday of your life.

You can reach that magic kingdom by choosing to live your life spiritually, following a path that originates from a deeper place within your mind and consciousness—your soul. To live from this place within your Spirit, you must commit to trusting the part of yourself that is intuitive, not logical. You must be ready to accept that your efforts to change your life and solve your earthly problems will work on an unseen level or plane of existence, and that you might not see immediate results. You'll be required to have faith, in yourself, your power, and the fact that the results of your efforts will manifest intangibly—first in the Spirit realm, before you see them happening in the material world.

Following a spiritual path, guided by the needs and desires of your soul, will bring you more satisfaction than you thought possible. You will become a fearless person, able to do things you never thought you could, to achieve your goals, and to be all you want to be.

A Reluctant Magician

If you are anything like me, and I am sure you are, there may come a time in your life when you realize that something is missing. You feel lonely, depressed, angry, and the future looks dark. You might be a person who makes lots of money, and things come easily to you, yet you still aren't happy. Your work no longer holds your interest, and the environment seems negative and oppressive. Or, you might be the person who struggles for every dime, never getting ahead. Whichever profile suits you, you are feeling what so many people are feeling today—that there must be a better way to live your life.

In the 1980s and early '90s I pursued my dream of performing on Broadway, using my master's degree in theater to support my acting and directing career with part-time college teaching positions. My years in the theater taught me so much about how to live from my Spirit. Rejection is a given in show business, and one's ego gets battered and bruised at every turn. You're never pretty enough, thin enough, talented enough, tall enough, etc., and sooner or later, it gets to you. Well, it got to me. There were days when my self-esteem was so low, I toyed with the idea of ending it all by my own hand. Miraculously, when I had had enough, I was divinely led to the discovery that if I focused my mind and my efforts, I could make things happen the way I wanted them to. The results were amazing!

My friend Becky had been an avid spiritual seeker for years, and introduced me to my spiritual potential. She guided me to books and people that made a remarkable difference in my life. I discovered meditation, a way of tapping into my own soul, and through it, a world of wonder, miracles, and magic opened up for me. I immediately began applying what I was learning about my innate divine power. Suddenly, unbelievable things happened.

I would go to auditions with the idea that I already had the job. Before I got there, and while I was waiting to go in to perform, I would affirm over and over again that I had this job, that they would love me, and that if I was divinely meant to have this part, I would get it. I stopped worrying about it, and began to trust that some higher power was helping me, so I decided to let that unseen assistant do its thing! Guess, what? I got jobs, lots of them! I actually started to make a living. That in itself was remarkable.

Everyday, I would put my spiritual plan of action to work before I did anything else, even before drinking that first cup of morning coffee. As the results began to manifest in my life, I found more power, more strength, more courage to trust completely in the invisible power that was guiding me. Following my path, I managed, in a very short time, to attract lucrative jobs, buy a brand-new car, pay off a huge credit-card debt of $30,000-plus, and get happy! That was the most remarkable result of all. A major attitude change occurred. I no longer felt helpless and hopeless; my depression lifted and I began to create a rich, loving, joyful, abundant, and prosperous life, because I truly believed I could!

Fight the Good Fight with Faith

If there is one thing I have learned moving along my own spiritual path, it is that you will stop yourself cold if you lose your faith—the unshakable belief that you are being guided to a mystical life in direct connection and communication with your Spirit, and that same Spirit exists in a Universe of all possibility. In my book *How to Get Everything You Ever Wanted: Complete Guide to Using Your Psychic Common Sense* (Llewellyn, 2000), I talked about the nuts and bolts of manifesting, drawing whatever you want into your life—money, love, good health, etc. In this book my goal is to focus on the tools that we all need to get our minds, hearts, and spirits ready not only to manifest, but to change ourselves into a spiritual fighting machine, able to do battle with negativity and our most debilitating emotions of rage, depression, and fear—and to win! To do this, we must be willing to throw off our old outmoded thinking, and place our entire lives in the hands of a force we generally cannot see, feel or touch. It requires great courage and an even greater commitment.

This is war, everyone, and your greatest enemy is yourself. Manifesting "stuff" is wonderful and something our Creator wants for us, but the stuff will have very little meaning to us once it is acquired, if we have not done the inner spiritual work that will help us make the best use of our acquisitions. Happiness is not about having a lot of possessions, or money, or fame. It is about what you do with all of that, to serve your Creator and the others that live on this Earth. Think "Oprah Winfrey," "Princess Diana," "Mother Teresa," or "Rosie O'Donnell" if you're having trouble grasping that concept. People who seem to have it all, and then use their wealth, notoriety, and influence in society to help others, are outstanding examples of what it means to be truly spiritual people. I am talking about a lifelong practice, a way to live in a constant state of joy, whether we get the stuff or not! That is magic. The pursuit of this contentment with life, inner peace, and satisfaction is a challenging undertaking that requires your constant attention. It's not for quitters. They don't call us "spiritual warriors" for nothing!

I can most definitely assure you that there is a way to live a magical life, because I have done it, myself. I am no different from you, and have no more power than you, yourself possess, right here, right now. You, too, can have a life full of all that you desire, and most importantly, one that raises your consciousness and enriches your Spirit. If you believe it, you can have it!

Take the First Step: Accept Your Greatness

In this first step, you need to face your life head-on and make a pivotal decision. I know it won't be easy, but it is necessary if you truly want to live your dreams. Dreams really do come true. *You must decide to accept that there is a power deep within the essence of your being that can change your life.* There is a part of you that is so strong and mighty it actually sends a vibration out into the universe that alters the events of your life, through the sheer force of your will. Yes, it seems too good to be true, but I am here as a living example of it, and I have helped many others find and use this power, too. It does require devotion and hard work, but the reward is far greater than the effort.

Years ago, I was teaching theater and speech at a private college in New York. There I met a very remarkable young woman. It was the first day of my public speaking class, and I was doing my customary orientation familiarizing the students with my procedures, reviewing the outline and assignments for the semester, and finally taking the roll. As I recited the names on the roster, I instructed the students to say, "Here," so that I could begin to associate names with faces. When I called one man's name, I heard a distinctively feminine voice respond. The woman identified herself as the wife of the student. Apparently, he had to work and miss this first class session, but she assured me that he would be present for all the subsequent classes. She asked if I would mind if she remained to take notes for him. I had no objection and proceeded with the remainder of my lesson plan.

During my second class session, taking the roll again, I called the previously absent man's name, and as he responded, I looked up to make my customary association of name-to-face. Surprisingly, I saw his wife sitting next to him. She asked if she might stay for the class, and if I would give her a moment of my time, afterward. I curiously agreed.

After class, the woman told me a story that appealed to the pushover in me. She said that as long as she could remember it had been her dream to go to college, but she didn't feel she could do it. She confided that as a child she barely made it through school, getting Ds and Fs, and that her parents were very disappointed in her. She carried this pain well into her thirties, and was totally convinced that she was not smart enough or capable enough to pass the courses, let alone graduate. I was so moved as she tearfully recounted her story and her feelings of inadequacy, I immediately proceeded to encourage her.

She was receptive when I told her that she had the power to succeed at school, or at whatever she pursued. I confided in her that I found a way to overcome my self-doubt and do the things I have always wanted to do, and that I was willing to share my plan with her if she was committed enough to take the first step. She agreed, so I asked her to put her faith in the part of her consciousness that had created the desire in the first place, her Spirit, because it would be her strength, and if she trusted it completely she would not fail. I explained that her dream was within her reach, and not to entertain any debilitating or self-defeating thoughts, to visualize and see herself joyfully accepting that degree on graduation day. In her youth, she had been inundated with negativity from her teachers and parents. I told her to forgive them all, and get busy putting to better use the energy she was wasting on anger for them and on hating herself.

I guess our talk impressed her, because the next day she made a simple request. She asked if I would allow her to attend my class as an observer. This process is called auditing, and usually must be okayed by the college administration, and a fee paid. I took a risk and let her stay. It was one of the most rewarding things I had ever done in my teaching career.

Over time, I shared my spiritual process with my "special student." The change in her attitude was the most interesting result of her inner work. She evolved from the beaten, sad woman I had met on the first day of class into someone who was willing to take chances to change her life.

Her newly found confidence demonstrated itself as the semester went on. When the students were about to make their first speeches, she came to me and asked if she could perform one! I was astounded by her courage. Not only that, she wanted to take all the tests, too! My intuition told me that this was surely a lesson for both of us, so I agreed.

Her enthusiasm, dedication, and talent exceeded that of many of the enrolled students. She even wanted me to grade her performance! I did so, unofficially, and by the end of the semester she had become an outstanding achiever, pulling an imaginary final grade of B+. Her joy was incredibly gratifying to witness, and I cry thinking of it to this day.

A final victory came for this brave young woman. She had one final request for me—would I write a note telling her now-aging parents what she had done, and what her grade would have been had she actually been enrolled? A "victory of the Spirit," I called it, when she visited me the following semester and ecstatically revealed that she had delivered the note, and found the courage to enroll. No one was more surprised with her transformation than she, she said. She admitted being a bit skeptical when I outlined my action plan for her, but, thinking that she had nothing to lose, she went for it. Four years later, her vision of proudly accepting her college degree became a reality, and she was well on the road to creating a life of magic. She stands as just one example of what we can do when we take the first step and accept our power.

"Double, Double,
Toil and Trouble . . ."

Hunched over a steaming cauldron, Shakespeare's mythical witches in his play *Macbeth* predict the tragedy that lies ahead for the hero because he is blind to his power to create and to destroy. What is the condition of your life, at this moment in time? What have you created or destroyed? If there is a void in your life, what is missing might not necessarily be material possessions, lovers, friends, or money, because you may well have all of these already. Your melancholy might be caused by your basic belief that you are a victim of the Universe, that something acts upon your life from outside of you and bestows upon you all that life has to offer, materially and spiritually, or deprives you of it. This is limited thinking. It is so limiting that it can, and most surely will, keep you from your joy and from creating a truly fulfilling life.

Your Magic Wand: Believe In
and Accept the Power

Your magic wand is your belief and acceptance of the power to create that exists within you. It is your belief and acceptance of God. That's what I call it, but you can call it whatever you like: Universe, Goddess, the Source, the Creator. It is all the same energy, that life force within us, which is always available and waits patiently for our bidding. To tap into this energy, you first have to abandon outmoded victim-like thinking and accept that it exists as fact. You must also accept responsibility for your life, and the recognition that you design all aspects of your own world. Ultimately, you live what you create. The blessed news is you don't have to do your creating alone.

When you understand and own that you are the primary architect of your life, that powerful thought sends a life-changing message to God/Universe, a prayer, if you will. That message/prayer lets the Universe know that you are now willing and open to working with the higher, spiritual level of your mind, your God-Mind, which can do anything without limit. You begin to look at life differently. You see promise in your future and you feel hope, an emotion that you previously thought was long-lost.

Embark On Your Enchanted Spiritual Journey

I am assuming that if you have gotten this far into the book you are ready to do some work. It has been my experience, and that of my students and clients, that opening the door to a new life requires a very simple effort. This effort is nothing more daunting than taking the time to sit quietly and reflect. Simply thinking about what you have read here, and what you truly want in your life will begin to shape and incite cosmic energy, and your process of growth will have begun.

Let's set the wheels to motion as we do the following simple reflection exercise. All it requires is your willingness. If you like, as you reflect you might want to jot down your thoughts in a journal. It is wise to dedicate a specific journal to your spiritual journey, and the insights you receive while reading and using this book.

Don't clutter and scatter your thoughts and energy by using the same journal for all your spiritual endeavors. Keep and title separate journals for all your pursuits, i.e., a Spiritual Journey Journal, a Dream Journal, a Manifesting Journal, etc. Don't let anyone read your journals. It is always wise to keep your own spiritual counsel. If you share your intimate thoughts and ideas when you are in the first stages of your work, you will dissipate their strength. Remember, the goal is to focus and build your power. There is plenty of time to share, once your life is effectively on its spiritual path.

Reflection 1

To Think, Perchance, to Dream . . .

This reflection has two parts. The first asks you to look back at what you have already created in your life. The second allows you to dream, to think about what you would have liked to create if you could go back and do it over. Don't reflect to the point that you drive yourself crazy trying to analyze yourself. Just relax with this process and let the thoughts surface that need to be aired. Make every effort to view them objectively, even though some strong emotions might arise when you do this work. Keep a box of tissues handy, just in case, and don't worry, this purging is really good for the soul. It helps you clear out that old pain and release it so you can move forward in your life, to your joy. Get ready to stop those nagging thoughts of doubt and replace them with constructive, healing energy. Believe, accept, and grow with the guidance and love of the power of Spirit within you! You can do this! Start now.

Part One

Allocate about fifteen minutes of your time to this reflection. Find a comfortable place to sit, upright in a chair or on a sofa, and place your feet flat on the floor. Your hands should be resting comfortably, palms either up or down on your lap, arms at your sides. Resist the urge to lie down, or lean your arms on those of a chair. These behaviors will either be conducive to your falling asleep during your reflection, or your arms could get "pins and needles" and distract you.

Now, close your eyes, take three gentle breaths, and relax. As you calm your mind, begin to reflect upon your life up to this point.

Allow your mind to go back in time to when you first began to feel frustrated with your life, or anxious, depressed, or angry at the path your life was taking. Try to pinpoint it.

Often, in this type of reflection, you will be surprised at when your dissatisfaction began. You might have thought that everything was fine then, but now that you look back at it, you might realize that you could have been ignoring the signs of discontent. The realization may clarify why you weren't completely happy or fulfilled, or why you might have felt anxious at that time in your life. This is very valuable information.

Look objectively at how you handled any crisis or disappointment that might have occurred at this time. Ask yourself, "How did I react, emotionally? What did I do about this situation? How did I handle it overall?"

This part of the reflection will take some time and effort, so don't rush the process. You might not be successful the first time you try it, but don't be discouraged, you may have a block in your subconscious mind that won't allow you to think about sad or upsetting times. It is necessary though, if you truly want to move past them, but your consciousness must be ready, so don't push it. Simply stop the exercise and try it again at another time.

Record any interesting information in your journal now. Try to write down as many details as you can re-member. You should also record how you felt when thinking about your life. Jot down your emotional responses, because they will tell you a lot about how you respond to negativity. Your emotional responses and perceptions might very well be the blocks you will need to overcome on your spiritual path to living a sacred life, or the lessons your soul will need to learn. It is not necessary to do anything with this information now. Just record it to refer to later on in your self-discovery work. Just the act of realization will trigger your soul's progress. Relax and let it happen.

Part Two

If you were successful with the first part of this reflection, go on to the next. Be sure to record any significant information in your journal before proceeding to this second part.

Now, give yourself the same amount of time, assume your comfortable position, close your eyes once again, relax, and take three gentle breaths. As you calm your mind, go back to the place in time that you have just discovered in Part One.

Allow your mind to recreate the events as you would have liked them to be. Change the scenario from an upsetting one into a positive, happy one. Fantasize and recreate the outcome.

You should be feeling satisfied and content with the new result. Go with these thoughts and think about what you might have done, or what could have been done differently to eliminate your negative or painful feelings.

As you look at this time in your life from a more positive perspective, ask yourself these questions, "What have I learned from this experience? What can I do differently in the future in similar situations? Looking back, how have I grown through having this experience? What good have I done, or will I do, that will help others facing a similar situation?"

You might not get all the answers to your questions at this point. The reflection is meant to exercise your mind, and to open it to progressive, constructive thought. Thought creates reality. If we can harness and focus our thoughts, we can create the reality we desire.

Once again, record your insights, feelings, and significant thoughts, and file them away in your journal for future reflection.

Receive the Magical Power of Your Soul

That's enough for now. You have done well simply by trying this reflection and doing as much of it as you could. You have sent a message to the Universe that you are willing and able to accept your life as it was, and as it can be, and are open to creating life anew. You have stated that you are, once and for all, committed to receiving God's blessings, and are ready to begin working with Spirit toward a new and exciting life. Receiving and accepting your power is one of the most important attitude changes you can make. Most people don't realize that even though they want a more spiritual and joyful life, they are really not willing to accept it on some level. The responsibilities are great when we live a life in service to our Creator and to others in the world. There may be a hidden reluctance to making such a serious commitment locked away in our psyche. That is why it is important to really be ready to set out on your sacred journey, with no doubts, fears, or anxieties. It takes a wholehearted willingness to put God first, above all things, and trust that He or She is a real, vibrant energy working in and through you. I think this is quite a major decision on your part, but let me assure you that once you have acknowledged the wonder and peace of Spirit within and around you, you'll never regret having made the choice. What you have accepted is not only the responsibility of living a spiritual life, but the opportunity for your soul to grow in enlightenment, and experience the magic of constant peace, joy, abundance, prosperity, and love.

Affirm the following with enthusiasm, and repeat until you *believe* it:

Affirmation 1

"I am open, ready, and willing to
accept the extraordinary power that
lies within me. Today, I take the first
step on my spiritual path and accept
my greatness. I replace all my old
negative beliefs about myself with
one positive thought—I am a limitless being with the power to create a
magical life! And so it is!"

When we begin our spiritual journey, it is really important to realize that there is no one set path to follow. We each must find our own personal way, and follow the sacred path that feels right and true for us. Expect that your choices might not match those of your family and friends, but it does not mean that they are wrong—they are just different. I have found that until we come to grips with what we believe is true for us, or what we *feel is right for us,* we are unable to live a happy life. In this second step, we face our truth by examining our own beliefs and the beliefs of others, synthesizing the information we have researched and gathered, and then resolving to actively put our chosen philosophy to work in our daily life. We do this by listening to the guidance that comes to us from within our hearts. In other words, we allow our intuition to gently nudge us toward our enlightenment. It does so by leading us to people, books, events, and experiences that help us decide what is right and true for us. In this

Step 2

Take Action

Seek your truth: find and follow the spiritual path that is right and perfect for you

way, we can better choose our most effective, and hence
true path to our Spirit.

How Does It Figure?

Many of us have quite a time trying to figure out what
our truth is. It is not as difficult as it appears. First you
must recognize what you believe in and then you need to
decide whether your beliefs still make sense to you after
you have examined them. A good deal of what we put our
faith in is not even our own thought. Our ancestors have
handed down religion, philosophy, art, culture, lifestyle,
and virtually every concept of living that we hold dear.
This is not a bad thing because we do need role models
and paradigms to follow in order to fashion our own
lives. Things get out of our reach when we come to rely on
those concepts already in place without further thought
or reflection. Think of what happens when racial prejudice is handed down from one generation to another. It
almost takes a rebellion to shake up outmoded or cruel
stereotyping. From the Civil War on down to the riots in
Los Angeles, we as a people have been rethinking the concepts that shape our lives, and we have been doing something about it.

Albeit, these are dramatic examples of rethinking, but
on a much more personal scale we must consider doing
the same if we wish to find our truth and embark on the
development of our spirit. Many times my clients and
church members have asked me how to begin to understand and deeply know their own individual belief system.
It was in answer to this question that I wrote this book.

If you follow a simple process of opening to your
highest good through prayer and affirmation, using the

techniques you read here, you will get to your spiritual goal. Just like anything else worth doing, it requires commitment and work. Notice I did not say hard work, because working on your spirit should not be perceived as a struggle. Granted, it is not an easy road because when you seek your own truth you are essentially going against the establishment, and that's no small task. Your family might think that you have lost your mind. Your friends might find you different or tell you you're "just not the same person anymore." Good. Maybe the person you truly are was compromised to suit other people, stronger people like parents, teachers, spouses, employers, or forceful friends. When you begin to live your way, you allow yourself to express your spirit, the most powerful part of your persona. Of course, this could mean that some of those folks who were around you may not like the new you, in which case you must bless them and let them find their own way, even if it means that they can no longer share your life.

What Is Truth?

This is a question I find worth pondering, in order to come to a realization of what is spiritually right for us as individuals. What is this personal truth that I am asking you to seek? It is the spiritual way of life you have created that reflects your personal connection with God, and through its practice, enables you to achieve your highest good, and equips you with the divine strength to live a loving life and help others to do the same. Imagine an individual personal belief system that empowers you to live an outstanding life and make remarkable contributions to the world. That is what it means to live your truth, but first you have to find it, understand it, and live it.

Seek and Find Your Way

To most people, truth connotes something that is factual—just and right—and cannot be disputed. How many of us as students have sweated our way through true or false questions on numerous tests? We were presented with only one choice—it was either right or wrong. Unfortunately, this is how many of us view our lives, as having the opportunity to make only one limited choice in all areas, situations, or problems that might arise. We then resign ourselves to having to live with the consequences, which many of us feel are more negative than positive. To some extent, this is what life seems to present, but the reality is that there is always more than one choice available to us at any given time. We live in an unlimited Universe. In such a place there is always more than one choice in every situation, and it is up to us to recognize those options. One of the keys to living our lives magically is the ability to accept that many choices exist, and then to make the best one for ourselves at that particular time. What has this got to do with truth, you say? Everything.

The choices you make directly reflect your belief system. Your belief system, simply defined, is what you believe to be true in your heart-of-hearts, from the essence of your being. It is your value system, the attitude you have about your life and how you feel you should live it. Every choice you make reflects your beliefs—it's that simple. Therefore, every choice you make either enhances or strengthens your belief system, or refutes and goes against it. Spiritually speaking, this means you are either making choices that feel right for you, or you are making choices that go against your very moral core. The results of the latter are uncertainty, doubt, and very often, emotional pain.

Let's look at some of these truths or beliefs that we humans tend to hold on to. When you read through the following list, you'll see that many of them are stereotypical and mythical.

Many of us humans seem to believe that:

- God is an energy that is outside of us, that controls us and our lives, and we can do nothing about it except pray and beseech.

- Life is tough. You just have to get through it until you die.

- Money is scarce, and real wealth is meant only for a chosen, select few.

- People are not to be trusted.

- Men only want one thing from women, and after they get it they leave you.

- Women want to change men, control them, and spend their money.

- I am a failure. Nothing I do works. I'll never amount to anything in this life.

- I hate myself. I'm too fat (thin, tall, short, stupid, smart, etc., you fill in the rest).

- You have to play the game in this life. It's a dog-eat-dog world, and the only ones who survive are the ones who know how to play the game.

- One needs to do whatever it takes to get ahead in this life, no matter who it hurts.

- I'm number one. If I don't watch out for myself, no one else will.

- Watch your back. There's always someone ready to stab you in it.

I could go on and on. After reading that list one could become very depressed. There are actually people who believe all of that negativity! And what's worse, they spew it out every chance they get to their families and friends. You know these people, and you might even admit to sharing some of these beliefs yourself. This attitude leads to sadness, depression, anger, resentment, and a lack of joy in living. Imagine how difficult it is to change that belief system, especially when it has been in place most of one's life. It's even been handed down from generation to generation! The more energy a person invests in this kind of thinking, the faster it becomes truth for them. So when a decision has to be made, it will come from this place of negativity instead of from a place of peace and harmony.

A person who holds these debilitating truths only has this basis of thought to use when faced with a crucial decision. Let us say that someone needs to make a choice between staying at a job that he or she hates or seeking out one that would be more enjoyable or that fulfills a secret dream. Based on the above beliefs, this person is likely to choose to stay at the dissatisfying job because, to quote:

- Life is tough. You just have to get through it until you die.

- Money is scarce, and real wealth is meant only for a chosen, select few.

- I am a failure. Nothing I do works. I'll never amount to anything in this life.

- I hate myself.

I think you get the idea. It's really important for us to take a good objective look at what we believe to be true in life and commit to changing our perspective, in order to create magic. Let me list the beliefs of someone who has decided that he or she is through with outmoded negative thinking, and is ready to take action and create new, more enlightened truth for him- or herself. Check out this belief system:

- God is part of me. I can do all things with this great power within. I can change my life for the better.

- The Universe is abundant. There is more than enough money for all of us. Wealth is my birthright. I attract money easily and always have more than I need.

- People are basically an aspect of God in human form, doing the best they can to make sense of this life. I attract only loving, trustworthy people into all areas of my life.

- Men are great. I attract only loving, spiritual, trustworthy men into all areas of my life.

- Women are great. I attract only loving, spiritual, trustworthy women into all areas of my life.

- I am a success in all that I do.

- I love myself, just the way I am, and I am lovable.

- Life is not a game, but rather a challenge to my Spirit. The world is full of opportunities to learn and grow. It is easy for me to survive and thrive in this world.

- To get ahead in this life, one only needs to serve God, other people, and all forms of living things, harming none.

- I'm number one, and I regard all others as I regard myself. If I care for others they will care for me. What I sow, I reap.

- I am safe in this world. I live a secure life.

What a difference. Let's pose the same question to our imaginary person, as we did above. The choice is to stay at a nowhere job, or not. With this new and positive belief system the decision most likely would be to leave the old position and to seek out one that is more spiritually satisfying because:

- God is part of me. I can do all things with this great power within. I can change my life for the better.

- The Universe is abundant. There is more than enough money for all of us. Wealth is my birthright. I attract money easily and always have more than I need.

- I am a success in all that I do.

- Life is not a game, but rather a challenge to my Spirit. The world is full of opportunities to learn and grow. It is easy for me to survive and thrive in this world.

This illustration should drive home the point of how very important it is to our spiritual, emotional, and physical well-being to examine our ingrained notions and establish new, productive truths for ourselves.

To further our soul's growth and find our spiritual path, we must also accept that truth is a very subjective concept, and that it is obviously different for everyone. There are as many belief systems as there are people in this world. No two are exactly the same, unless of course someone is brainwashed by a mysterious cult. Our society encourages us to make choices that are in keeping with what it feels is right and just, adding pressure to our decision making. For instance, having been raised in New York City, the question of finding parking spaces is a big deal to most people because there are so few of them. Here you are on your way to the theater and you are amazed that you find a parking space within walking distance! What you don't see is the sign posted on the next block that says parking is prohibited there. After all, others are parked there so it must be okay. When you return from enjoying the show, you find your car has been towed to the pier detention center, and it will cost you $150.00 to get it out! What happened?

This scenario did happen—to me. I reasoned, "There was no sign on that block, so I thought it was fine to park there." That was the statement of truth I made to the officer who impounded my vehicle and would not return it to me without a check for $150.00, but I was telling the truth. Unfortunately, it was not his truth. His truth was that I parked in a forbidden zone. Period. His truth told him that although the sign was not posted on that block, drivers were expected not to park until they came to a sign listing the legalities. Whose truth prevailed? It wasn't mine.

What I learned from this experience was that we were both right. Truth is relative. Truth is what you believe it to be, regardless of what the other guy thinks. This is big news. In that situation I had to pay a fine, but I wasn't necessarily wrong, nor was I right. My lack of information about the city's parking rules caused me to form a truth that didn't match the situation, but what I gleaned from the experience was worth the $150.00. I learned to stop fighting with people over what truth is. The truth is gray, not black and white, and it is by all means subjective.

Get Moving!

"So, what are you saying here?" you ask. I am saying that in order to live spiritually, joyfully, and productively, we must rethink our definition of truth, accept it, and then we must make the necessary choices to actively live our personal truth each day of our lives. We need to get moving on this path. Once we begin to recognize the spiritual signposts along our path, we must follow them and put into daily practice what we are learning, all the while accepting that others are doing the same. What is true for you is not necessarily true for everyone else. Having said that, this second step should guide you to clarify what truth is for you and help you to begin living each day doing the things you believe will lead you to your ultimate joy. Recognizing the spiritual principles that work for you, what feels right to you, will help you pinpoint the actions you must take to guide you to a way of living that is not based upon negative thinking or other people's notions. Magic happens when you take action to seek and find your own personal truth, your own way to live that is kind, loving, and considerate of all life. More importantly, you must accept responsibility for your choices as you move along your sacred path.

The Devil Did It!

Sometimes we get tired of people telling us that what happens to them is not their fault. It is always someone else who is responsible for their bad luck, broken heart, ill health, or whatever. In their minds the truth is that they had nothing to do with whatever befalls them. I guess God or the Devil did it to them. Mind you, this theory applies only if what occurred is bad. If it's good, then they accept total credit. This scenario is the picture of someone giving over his or her power, surrendering individuality, and most of all blaming others for his or her choices. Many of these people find their way to my office. While I totally understand their thinking, nonetheless it is difficult to help them see and understand the beliefs at the core of their responses. One client said that she refused to take responsibility for what God had done to her! Her thought was that there was an overpowering force acting upon her life without her consent, and that she had no control or power over it. She was convinced of this beyond the shadow of a doubt. It was truth to her, based probably upon some of those negative beliefs I have listed before. She refused to take responsibility for her life, and therefore refused to take any constructive action to change it. Being a victim was easier than changing her truth. She could have replaced her negative thinking with the idea that she was powerful enough to direct the course of her life, and stop the unhappy events from occurring. To this day, she still wholeheartedly believes in the victim-ization-by-God concept as her truth. The sad part is that she is not alone. What is your truth about God? Are you willing to accept that changing your perception could change your life for the better?

Spirit Who?

God is known by many names. In this book you'll see references to God as Spirit, Universe, Source, Creator, etc. Spiritual seekers want to understand what this thing called God is, and we want, even more eagerly, to form a relationship with this divine energy! We are actively in search of our own spiritual truth. I don't know about you, but I don't want the relationship with Spirit that my God-blaming client has. My truth about this force of good in the world is quite simple. I believe that God is within and all around us, that we are connected to Spirit by our very nature, our soul, and that we, other people, animals, plants, other planets, and life-forms, are all part of this same energy, which is love. I believe God, and therefore we, are limitless, that the Universe is a loving and abundant place, and we are here to serve God in all of its aspects, and to learn and grow our spirit. I arrived at this truth over time, in pursuit of my own spiritual journey. This belief becomes stronger in my consciousness with each passing day. As I pursue my writing, teaching, healing, and counseling work, every blessed activity continues to enrich and expand my soul. I have changed my limiting beliefs and found my truth. Not only have I realized what works for me, I have taken an active part in changing the circumstances of my life and my environment to reflect my beliefs. That has made all the difference!

Do Your Thing

Our world is abundant with spiritual, religious, and philosophical options. There are all sorts of belief systems to espouse, rituals to perform, and texts to imbibe. I suggest that we forget about all of them for a time, and work our way through that maze to the heart of our personal beliefs. We must challenge ourselves to examine what motivates, moves, and inspires us, decide to accept these concepts, and then actively incorporate them into our lives. This is the second step in living a magical life.

First, we need to explore other beliefs in order to decide what does or doesn't work for us. We need to discover what gets our spiritual juices flowing, what fires up our enthusiasm and propels us toward living a full and exciting life. It is necessary to wade through the melange of doctrine and dogma to a place of calm, quiet, and truth within us. I'm not trying to tell you that all religion is a sham, by any means. What I am trying to say is that religion is only a tool to finding what is really spiritual in your life. Established philosophies are simply collective thoughts and decisions that other people made for us. They are valid and necessary in that they provide us with the impetus to care about our souls. Think about that. Without religion we would not, as a species, be the least bit concerned with our eternal selves. Do animals care as much as we do about God? Intellect forces us to question, and when we do, our confusion requires answers. Religion answers to our confusion and allays anxiety. This might have been really effective in the first century, but in the twenty-first we're looking for something more!

There are plenty of our fellow humans ready to provide us with a new way—their way. You might be thinking about me, "She wrote this book. Doesn't she want us to believe what she says is true?" No. I don't. I ultimately would hope that you would use this book, or any other, as a tool, an instrument, a point of reference, from which you can begin to form your own truth. We have experienced the rise of cults in America, attracting seemingly intelligent, capable people, yet who will react with violence if someone invades their territory. My point is that we can buy into anything if it is presented well. Television commercials shape consumer commerce, and the media tries and convicts. All this is done only too well. What can we make of the rhetoric? Is it all truth? Yes.

Second, after taking an objective look at the many spiritual options that exist in our world, developing a clear vision of what God means to us, what motivates and inspires us, and what the goals of our soul appear to be, places us in a position to accept this synthesis of ideas as our personal truth.

Third, when we have decided what path our soul wants to take we must commit to actively incorporate our beliefs into our everyday life. When you live your truth by making daily choices that reflect it you will see remarkable changes in the way you deal with problems and difficult people. You'll see that you no longer hold others responsible for your circumstances and you can be tolerant of their choices, good or bad, because you understand that life is merely a reflection of our thoughts.

When you take action to find your path, commit to it, and then live it actively each day, you become an omniscient observer of all that is happening in your world. You participate in life around you as it is deemed necessary, but you are able to live happily and magically because you are removed from it. You are in the world but not of it. Sounds biblical, doesn't it? It's true. Establishing a certain distance from the world does not mean that we no longer care what happens to the underprivileged, sick, homeless, or war-stricken. It means that we become objective. We no longer take to heart everyone's truth as our own. We do what is necessary to find and live our own way, reverent to the Earth and all forms of life upon it, assisting others, and sharing when and where we are needed. Living this way requires that we take responsibility for what we believe, and not just blindly accept the teachings of one leader, church, or philosophy over another, without first defining whether or not it really rings true for us.

A Word of Warning: Dodge the Bullets

Seeking your truth demands that you recognize what is important to you in this life, and then act upon it. What is even more important is that whatever you do, you do it without causing harm, judgment, or any form of negativity to others who don't accept your definition of what truth is. In other words, you may have to dodge a few bullets! Your chosen philosophy may not be what the world, or your mother, is ready to accept. When you set out to live your truth and travel your spiritual journey, you will encounter some bumps along the road. There will always be someone who thinks you're wrong and will tell you so! You must do your best to remain true to yourself, while bobbing and weaving through the maze of opposing viewpoints you will no doubt face in your work.

When I first hung out my shingle as a metaphysical intuitive counselor and minister, I got a few very upsetting phone calls. People would call my office and leave terrible messages. It seems they didn't have the courage to speak to anyone in person. Rather, they left a few choice words telling me that I was going to hell, and so was anyone else whom I ensnared into my devil's den. They never identified themselves or left a number where they could be reached for further comment.

This kind of thing persists today, six years later. Just recently, an unidentified man paid a visit to my office. Seeing that it was closed, he entered the neighboring office and began to question the women who worked there, sarcastically phrasing, "Just what are they doing in there?" The ladies were so spooked by him they refused to answer his inquiries. Their later observations to me were that they got a bad feeling around him.

Needless to say, the truth of all of these people does not match mine. Yet, if what I have said is valid, then we as spiritual seekers must not retaliate. We must accept the attackers spiritual truth as their own, and neither place judgment nor blame. So, seeking your truth doesn't just mean that you find your own thing and do it; it means you respect that others are doing the same. We need to continue to act in accordance with the spiritual path that we have chosen. Sometimes, it just isn't easy!

Following your path also implies that you do not require others to live up to your spiritual expectations, and learn to accept that others might not be as far along on their path as you are. For instance, in addition to the obvious examples above, there is another type of person who is not quite sure of their spiritual path, but quick to criticize yours. They are harder to spot, but you know these people. They go to services in their church or temple of choice every weekend, but during the week they conveniently forget what they believe in. These folks pick and choose from certain parts of the religious dogma they claim to profess. Then they give lip service to the particular principle when it serves them. They like some parts of their religion, and ignore others. Some of these believers even fight for particular doctrines and then hypocritically reject others.

For instance, I know of people in my own life and experience who actively oppose abortion. They believe it to be murder, and even support those who would violate the civil rights of others to the point of murdering doctors—all this in the name of God. Then they think nothing of having an extramarital affair, or using chemical birth controls, clearly against the same faith that outlaws abortion. Let's just say that these people are not clearly on a spiritual path. They are so confused by what they feel they *should* believe, because that's what nice boys and girls do, that they are experts in denial, and in the end go ahead and do what they really *want* to do, religion or no religion.

When you take spiritual action and live your truth, you do not need to find validation in any religion. You find it inside of you. Religious practice becomes a healthy tool of expression, rather than a crutch. Your soul becomes real to you and you intuitively know that there is a God and that God is within and all around you. There is no desperate need to force others to think as you do, no anger exists, and all that we feel for each other, regardless of what truths we may believe, is love—love beyond belief.

Living True to the Grand Plan

As I have said, this journey to find the real you need not be a struggle, but at times it can present us with difficult decisions. That is part of the plan. The plan that I'm talking about is the grand scheme of your life, the purpose of your existence, the reason why you came to Earth. You and God/Spirit/Goddess/Universe, etc., decided long before you were born what you would learn while you were here, whom you would work with on your path, your genetic makeup, the parents you would have, and all the events, joyful and sad, that would help you to find your way back to the greatness from which you came. Of course, this is the basic concept of reincarnation; that we have come back to this planet in different forms and in different lifetimes so that we could learn and grow in our godliness.

The concept of reincarnation seems to explain why most of us have such an urge to "find ourselves," if you will pardon the cliché. Intuitively we know that there is more to our "self" than meets the eye. We find our genuine self by working toward our spiritual goals in this lifetime, and by living truthfully. As we move through this life, we learn our lessons through tough times and happy times, and we learn how to live in flow with our nature, the part of ourselves that is at peace and calm, and in harmony with others, animals, the environment, and all energies extant in the universe.

Take the Next Step: Action!

The title of this step is *Take Action*, so take action we shall! The only way to find out what you are all about, your personal truth, is to think about it, reflect upon it, and allow it to make its way to your conscious mind. The fact is that your spirit knows its truth already, but your consciousness might not. In other words, you have all the answers you need right now; you're just not aware of them. We have all had those moments when we are discussing an important topic with someone, and we say something so profound it astounds us. Your response might be, "Wow, where did that come from?" It was there all along, hiding. Your subconscious mind has lots of those gems locked away in it that your Spirit retains and unleashes when you least expect it, so that you can be spurred on to keep searching. God has a way of letting us know just what we need to know, and only at those particular times when we need to know it—not one minute sooner. It keeps life interesting.

Let's get moving and continue the process toward understanding and living a magical life by working on the following reflection.

Reflection 2

The Truth Be Known!

As with all the reflections in this book, you do not have to do all the sections of them at once. Read through them all first, and then decide which you would like to address. Prioritize. Not all of us will need to reflect on all the concepts I've listed here. Use what you need. This is your magical journey, so design it your way, and make your own magic.

As you did in Reflection 1, allocate about fifteen minutes of your time for this exercise. Find a comfortable place to sit, upright in a chair or on a sofa, and place your feet flat on the floor. As before, your hands should be resting comfortably, palms up or down, as you like, on your lap, arms at your sides.

Now, close your eyes, and take three gentle breaths, and relax. Feel a wave of relaxation moving from the top of your head, all the way down to the tips of your toes. Now, reflect upon the following questions:

> *Whom do you most admire as a person? In your perception, how does he or she live their life? What do you feel are this person's beliefs, and how do you see those beliefs demonstrated in the things this person does and says? How do they treat others? What characteristic is it you most admire about them, and wish you could develop in yourself?*

With this first section you are on the road to self-discovery. We often choose friends and mates or admire those who embody the characteristics that we feel lacking in ourselves. It is called *complementarity*. We try to associate with others who complement our own personality, and supply those qualities that are missing in ourselves. The idea here is to recognize those qualities and develop them in ourselves so that we become the person we want to be. We will still want others in our lives, but when we find our own truths, we no longer depend on them for our happiness.

Now allow your mind to think about what inspires you. What writers, spiritual figures, religions, or philosophies seem to make sense or resonate with you? Which do not? Ask yourself why. Let your mind fully expand on these basic belief systems, and deeply examine what you feel is fair and just to all people within these systems. Your intuitive mind will gently lead you, and you will find that you will know what repels or attracts you to a certain person or philosophy. Keep in mind that if you feel a strong emotion arise within you during this reflection it is a significant message from your higher self, so pay close attention to it. Try to understand the basis of the emotion and remain open to your intuitive perceptions.

The above section of this reflection will help you decipher how you feel about your current religious beliefs and the spiritual leaders/founders/icons of that religion. The emotional response will help you. It is your indicator that you are on the right track or not, and will help you to decide what action you need to take on your journey. In keeping with that idea, the following section will help you understand what you believe are your strengths and how to see them as enhancements to your life.

Gently allow your mind to relax and think about what you like to do. What are your talents and abilities? What hobbies do you enjoy? What would you like to share of those talents with others? How can you use them to make a difference in other people's lives, as well as your own, or in the world at large?

Record any interesting information in your journal now. Again, as before, try to write down as many details as you can, as well as your emotional responses.

Tried and True for You

Congratulations! You have now examined your basic inner truths. You have allowed your mind to analyze what seems comfortable, right, and fair to you, as it is seen in the philosophies that exist now, and through the lives of those people you most admire. You have even given yourself permission to pat yourself on the back and take an objective look at your talents and abilities, and how they might be used to contribute to our society.

Having done your inner work, you are now ready to get out into the world and take action to find the path that makes you happy and gives you a sense of connectedness to your Creator, and all of life. You'll do this by weeding through all the spiritual mumbo jumbo out there, deciding upon the spiritual philosophy that is right and perfect for you, and then making a heartfelt commitment to yourself to live your beliefs each day. And then, my friend, you will be well on your way to living your magical life.

Affirm the following with enthusiasm, and repeat until you *believe* it:

Affirmation 2

"I now commit to seeking my own personal truth. I let go of old notions and open my heart, allowing what is true for me to express itself throughout every area of my life. I take definite action in the pursuit of my divine plan and my highest good. And so it is!"

There is an ancient saying: "When the student is ready, the teacher comes." I cannot emphasize how true this is. In my own life I have been guided to the right people at the precise moment I needed them. This is no coincidence. If you believe that your life is spiritually guided, then you will have no trouble understanding that the Universe silently engineers us into the path of those who can do the most good for our soul's growth. Spiritual teachers and mentors exist in all forms, seen and unseen. We must accept this fact and actively set out to look for them. Allow your consciousness to be open to the perfect teachers for your unique journey. In pursuing this, the third step on your path, you must become aware of the presence of your teachers, look for them and seek them out, turn to your intuition to tell you if this teacher is right for you, and explore the possibility of contacting supernatural energies to help and guide you along the way.

Your spiritual mentors, those who are destined to help you find and stay

Step 3

Find Your Teachers

Open your heart and mind to your spiritual mentors

on your path, may come to you formally in the form of earthly teachers, such as myself and other authors, speakers, clergy, yoga, tai chi, or meditation instructors. They may find their way to you through friends, newspapers, magazines, advertising flyers, posters, billboards, etc., but rest assured that they will appear just when you need them. You'll be in a bookstore and all of a sudden you'll see a title that interests you and you'll say to yourself, "I was just thinking about that. I wanted to find out more about that subject, and here it is! How do you like that?" You will amaze yourself. The fact is that you are actually attracting the book through your thoughts. They are very powerful. Desire is behind them, and when desire is coupled with determination, there is no stopping you! You become irresistible to the positive forces in the Universe, and presto—you get what you need just when you need it! It's magic, remember. But, as always, it is up to you to pay attention to the signs and take the necessary steps to advance your learning. As you actively search for your teachers, keep in mind that they are our kindred spirits, and won't be that hard to find. After all, they have been "waiting" for us. They are those special souls whose spiritual mission or life purpose is to lead us to our greatness.

Earthly Magicians

Master teachers are the highest level of teacher to have graced the Earth. They have been known throughout the ages. Jesus Christ, Buddha, and Mohammed all have been with us to awaken us to our own power and the limitlessness of the Universe. In our lifetime, we have seen greatness in many social and political leaders, in saints, and in the likes of human advocates, as I call them, such as His

Holiness the Dalai Lama, Ghandi, Mother Teresa, and Princess Diana. There have been those who have taught us how to revere and respect the Earth's environment and animals, and those who have taught us to relax, pray, rejoice, exercise our bodies, and even build a house. Read about these masters, read their works, and find others who can teach you about them. Their lessons are priceless.

As you work on this step, think about your other earthly teachers, maybe not as profoundly evident, but equally as important. They could have been those formal schoolteachers you encountered while you attended grade school, high school, or college. You may have liked some of them, or you may have disliked some of them. Either way, they not only taught the ABCs, but they also taught you something about yourself that you needed to learn at that time. The teachers we didn't like might have taught us the most about ourselves: how to value our thoughts, ideas, and opinions, and how to tolerate the negativity of others. Regardless of your feelings about them, they have helped shape your understanding of life.

Your informal earthly teachers may come to you in unusual ways. Several of my own students have told me how they found me. A few said that they had read an article I wrote for a local newspaper and were drawn by its message. Others were introduced to my classes through friends who had already been working with me. Still others found me in the phone book! When it is right, the invisible match is made.

Look for Your Teachers Everywhere

Some earthly teachers are harder to recognize because they do not come to us in the traditional guise. We are constantly learning with every breath we take, and therefore we are continually attracting events, situations, and people that force us to look at ourselves or our lives in a new way.

For instance, we often see our own foibles reflected in others. I have had many clients who have expressed exasperation at the number of negative people around them. One client in particular used to lament about her friends who did drugs, drank, and freeloaded at her house all the time. She described how unreliable they were and how they took advantage of her generous spirit by never bringing anything to eat or drink to her home, yet they thought nothing of eating and drinking her paychecks away. This woman had so much to learn, and the Universe sent her the perfect teachers—her self-absorbed friends! I told her to take a long, objective look at herself, because she was a mirror of them. Of course, this did not sit well with her. She was angry that I suggested that she was just like them, but being like them was part of her lesson.

The lady was attracting unreliable friends because of some need within her. Her soul required these people in order to place her in an uncomfortable life situation so that she would learn what she needed to know about herself and improve her life. Stress and negativity are cosmic wake-up calls, letting us know that change is necessary. I asked her if she also took drugs and drank, and she admitted so. It was clear she was attracting friends and lovers who were just like her. This was a difficult realization for her, because she was a very angry person, prone to blaming others for her problems. The fact that she was uncomfortable with these folks and wanted something different for herself was a spiritual gift. The discomfort was Spirit's way of letting her know that she had the power to change. When she began to change her habits for the better and made attempts to understand her lessons, the old self-destructive friendships began to fall away. Her friends stopped freeloading because she wouldn't accommodate them any longer. She stopped using drugs and drinking. She became aware of her lifestyle and she didn't like what she saw. It's no fun being sober in a bar with a lot of drunken people. Her life began to change for the better. She began meditating and joined my metaphysical church. There she met people who were sweet, loving, and drug-free.

What happened was really simple. When she began to change there was no longer a need for the former friendships, so they naturally fell away. Her unlikely teachers taught her much about herself, and when she no longer needed their instruction, having learned her lessons, they and she moved on. She opened her life to finding new friends. Some of her new lessons with her new teachers/friends were about loyalty, love, and nurturing.

So you see that some of the earthly magicians who help us transform our lives come to us in subtle ways. It is a very important job of ours to recognize them when they present themselves, and to understand that we will, by virtue of our human destiny, continue to attract them in order for us to continue along our spiritual path and expand our consciousness.

Be Aware of the Unseen Wizards

The true wizards of the Universe, in my humble opinion, are those teachers whom we cannot see. They are our celestial helpers, sometimes known as guardian angels, and they are ready and willing to come to our assistance. Get comfortable with that and let them know what you need. They're listening. We know that God/Universe/ Spirit is the overarching energy that guides our lives, and meta-physicians believe that this Force has created angels in order to get us humans out of some tough scrapes. After all, we can make a mess of things sometimes.

We have heard much about the presence and interven-tion of angels in recent years. Tracing history, we read about them in the roots of early Christianity, as they her-ald the coming of joyous events, and about their mysteri-ous power to assist humans. I could cite many instances of angelic appearances, but what is important for our purposes is that angels are teachers, too. When we con-nect with our angelic helpers we learn how to live a life of compassion and unconditional love. It is up to you to take this third step, and make that connection.

In my intuitive counseling practice, I have held angel channeling sessions in which a group of four people con-vene with the intention of contacting their angels. There are many sessions like this that you may attend, and books you can read that will acquaint you with these celestial helpers. In my own sessions, when we have prayed and meditated and called upon angels they have always made their presence known. I recall one evening when I realized that more than just a visit occurred. Pro-found learning had happened for one of the participants.

As we sat together calling the name of her angel, one woman began to sob uncontrollably. She was not the type of person to be overcome easily with tears, so we were all shocked when it happened. Through her tears she described that as we invoked the name of her angel she felt as though her body was being hugged gently. In her words she uttered, "I feel like wings are around me, and that I'm being hugged in the most loving way. I think this is unconditional love. I've never known it before." And with that she continued to weep with joy. She had been abused as a child and had never been close to her parents, feeling all the time that she was a mistake of nature, unwanted and unloved. For the first time in her life, she knew what it must be like to be special, valued, and loved just for herself. With her revelation the rest of us in the group began to cry, thrilled that she finally learned what a blessed soul she was.

This woman's angel taught her so much that day, without even saying a word. Angels will demonstrate their love to you in any number of ways, but one common thread among all of the angel happenings I have researched is that when one is visited by an angel, there is no doubt about it. After the incident, a person knows only too clearly that something miraculous has happened, and is ready to tell the world. I suppose that's what the angels have in mind, don't you think?

In my own life I have learned much from angels. They have been known to save lives, rescue us from dangerous encounters (I describe one of my own, as well as others, in my book, *How To Get Everything You Ever Wanted*), appear out of nowhere in human as well as animal form, and disappear in the blink of an eye. But what we learn from them in whatever form they come and whatever they do for us, is that we are more important to God than we think we are. Angels remind us that even what seems trivial in our lives, compared to the tragedies of others, is still important and worthy of God's attention.

Several years ago, I was performing at a benefit Christmas concert for the hospice organization in Stamford, Connecticut. When the weather changes, I tend to get sick. I don't know why, I just think that I need a vacation by that time of the year and my system goes on the fritz. Anyway, I had come down with a bout of laryngitis, unable to talk, let alone sing in my usual high soprano voice. My fellow performers and I were rehearsing for the show the evening before and hoping that I would, by some miracle, get my voice back. The fact is, all I could do was squeak! I called my friend Carol Kelly, who chairs this annual fundraising event, and told her I'd be okay, and I'd be there. Poor Carol didn't need this on the eve of the performance, but I assured her I'd be all right.

She probably didn't get much sleep that night and neither did I, because when I awoke the next day, I still had no voice. This is when I called in the heavy artillery, and started to pray. I am a trooper, having learned from my thirty or so years as a performer, never to "let 'em see 'ya sweat!" and of course, I was determined to go on stage that day, one way or the other, so I began affirming in my squeak-sound, "Thank you, God, for my singing voice back in perfect form, now. Thank you for enabling me to sing beautifully today. And so it is!"

As I dressed and got ready to go to the performance, I thought about how crazy this must seem to the other performers. Here I can't even talk, had no rehearsal, and yet

I'm still showing up for this! I had to use all the faith I could muster to get me there, hoping and repeating that God would get me through this insanity. When I arrived, Carol was beside herself when she heard me speak. "How are you going to sing?" she pleaded. "Just introduce me, and I'll be fine," I whispered, not knowing what would happen when I stepped up to the microphone.

The time had come. The introduction was made, everyone crossed their fingers, and I heard the pianist begin the introduction to my music, "I Believe." I took a breath and willed my voice to sing, and miraculously it did! I sounded better than ever! My fellow performers, Carol, and I were all stunned when I finished the number. For a moment we all looked at each other in disbelief. Carol stepped up to the mic and announced to the five hundred or so audience members that one second prior to that song, I had laryngitis! The entire place began to applaud and hoot! What a moment!

Now, you might be saying, "But what about the angels here? Isn't this section about angels?" Yes it is. I gave you the whole story because I learned one of the most powerful lessons of my life that day. The message was delivered by an angel.

Let's jump back for a moment to the end of my song, and Carol's announcement. After the performance, I left the stage, making my way among the crowd at the subsequent reception, heading for a cup of tea, when a gentleman stopped me. He was an older man in his 70s, I thought, with lovely snow-white hair and a pleasant, smiling face. He was wearing a beautiful black tuxedo. I thought that was unusual, because while this affair is attended by some of Connecticut's governmental officials and upscale community leaders, no one ever wears a tuxedo. It's not that kind of affair, not that formal.

When I got past the man's attire, I focused on what he was saying to me. He told me that I sang beautifully, like an angel, and that I should not have been so worried about it. He said that God had heard my prayer when I asked that my perfect singing voice be restored. I was stunned. How did he know what my prayer was? He practically repeated it word for word, and I had told no one! How did he even know I prayed? I could have been an atheist. We were total strangers, the man and I. Then he said something really amazing. He asked me why I had doubted that God would answer my prayer, even for a moment. Didn't I realize that God wouldn't let me down? The reason I was bowled over by this statement, was because I had entertained doubt. I had just *hoped* that God would give me my voice back. I didn't really *know* it would happen. Overwhelmed, I just looked at the man and we gazed at each other in silence. It seemed time stood still for a moment. I knew something outstanding was going on there. This man, this complete stranger, was teaching me about faith—my faith, or lack of it. He broke our silence and thanked me for a lovely performance, then walked away.

I stood deep in thought for a moment and then ran over to my friend, Jeff, who was performing with me that day. I asked if he had seen the old man because I wanted to point him out to Jeff and tell him about the incident. He said he saw no one, in a tuxedo, no less. Everyone would have noticed that. I ran around asking waiters and other guests if they had known or seen him. He couldn't have gotten past the ushers and coat check folks at the door, because he was old and couldn't run out that quickly. I even asked Carol, who oversees the invitations, and she didn't know who he was either. Then it hit me—he had disappeared as quickly as he had come. I had been the only one who saw or talked with him, and most importantly, I felt that my life had been changed forever. The mark of an angel!

All I can tell you is, if you are sincere about wanting to find your spiritual path, and as determined as I to open my heart to the greatness of the Universe, this kind of angel magic is unavoidable. When you make the effort to reach out to them, they will come to you, you will know them, and you will learn. This I know to be absolute truth, and you will never be the same again.

More Magicians!

As if angels weren't enough, the Universe/God has provided us with even more magic to aid us on our way. Other magical beings we can depend upon for assistance are our spirit guides. As is the case with angels, spirit guides have a mission. Our guides have lived one or more lifetimes with us, and are our soulmates. We and they have agreed that one of us will come to Earth and live another life, while the other remains in the unseen realm assisting us from there. What a deal, right? But, when you really think about it, we're the crazy ones for coming back. Our spiritual buddies are in bliss! That's why we need their help. We have returned to our Earth school to learn more lessons, and resolve old ones (karma), but we are not abandoned by our Creator. God has given us our spirit guides to help us get through the tough times with wisdom and peace, and we can have a conversation with them everyday!

Roger Smythe

I was enjoying a weekend retreat at the New Jersey shore, when, while playing a corny fortune-telling game, I heard a voice. The voice was clear and audible, as though it were speaking to me within the room, yet there was no physical body attached to it. I had heard about disembodied spirits making contact with those of us on Earth, but why me? So, just like any respectable human, I thought I was nuts! I was very frightened, but soon relaxed. It felt "right," in a strange sort of way.

Roger Smythe introduced himself as a spirit who had lived with me in another lifetime. He said we were actors together in London, in the 1800s, and that we were very close friends. He said that he had been with me as my spirit guide since my birth, and that we had a lot of work to do together. I didn't know what that work would be, because I was a starving actress and thought that the theater would be my life. Little did I know that sitting at this computer, pouring out my thoughts, would be it—my purpose for living! Roger told me that I would, from that day forward, see the rapid development of my psychic gifts. He was right, and my life has been one of wonder, joy, and magic, ever since.

Not everyone gets to meet their guide in such a remarkable way. Most of us are made aware in more subtle ways. We have a thought we can't shake, or a song keeps repeating itself in our head, or we physically perceive a pressure in our stomach area when we need to make a crucial decision. These are all ways in which our guides communicate with us. They may deliver messages to us through another person, such as a psychic or trance channel, in addition to making direct contact with us through our own thoughts, intuition, or gut feelings. These energies are ready and willing to help us whenever we call upon them. Their business is more on the day-to-day level, giving us guidance as to everyday decision making, such as which road to take to work, or what career would be most harmonious for us. Learn as much as you can about them, and learn to communicate with them. I have listed some helpful titles in the bibliography of this book, but you can begin now to contact your celestial helpers by doing the reflection exercise at the end of this chapter. Whatever you do, don't ignore them. Your guides want to help, so call upon them. You'll be glad you did!

Even More Magicians!

As if that weren't enough, there are even more heavenly energies waiting to assist us in this life. Our loved ones who have passed over into spirit are also there to help. If you have a loved one on the other side who was particularly close to you, your love will continue to draw them and keep them close. They have not abandoned you now that they are in spirit, and you can contact them for help when you need it, as well as for guidance along your path.

As a child growing up Catholic in the Bronx, New York, I had the gift of a dear parish priest and teacher, Father Tim Fiorello. Father Tim was known for his way with a story. He conducted the children's Mass every Sunday morning at 9:00 A.M. I couldn't wait to hear his sermons, always full of interesting parables that enthralled us children, to the point that we didn't even realize we were getting expert spiritual guidance. He had a way of "back-dooring" God, thereby keeping his pint-sized parishioners awake. I saw him again, almost forty years later, when he said the funeral Mass for my 100-year-old grandmother, Lena. In his loving, inimitable way, he expressed his unique wisdom when he said, "She is not gone. She has simply changed her address!"

Even though our loved ones have "changed address," they can still hear our prayers and perceive our loving thoughts of them. Some of them have actually decided to make charges of their loved ones still remaining on the Earth, acting as guides, and staying close to advise and protect.

All celestial energies, as well as those who have passed on, can be of help to us, even if we do not know them personally. If a composer needs help writing a song, he or she may call upon his or her favorite composers in Spirit. Imagine getting help with your tunes from Mozart, Beethoven, and Brahms! How about Jerry Garcia, Jim Morrison, or Janis Joplin? Taking a psychology test? Send a vibe out to Sigmund Freud or Carl Jung. Want to make a million? Call Howard Hughes!

This help is truly available to us. Remember, when we cross over into Spirit, the energy of our lifetime does not get destroyed. It simply returns to the collective consciousness, the energy that is in all of us. It is because of this phenomenon that we can call upon these people. Their energy in all of its power still exists within the universe. We humans have to make a huge effort to ignore all of this free assistance, and unfortunately, many of us do. Think about the folks you know who think this is all a lot of hooey. Their skepticism may forever keep them from utilizing the abundance of support that is right at their beck and call.

Let's get past any of our own doubt with the next reflection. Doing it will open the door to your receiving and drawing to yourself your earthly and unearthly spiritual teachers.

Reflection 3
Calling All Teachers!

The results of this reflection and the affirmation that ends this chapter will be quite dramatic when they are done faithfully and with enthusiasm. You are about to put out a major call to Spirit/Universe for your guidance. Do not take this lightly. This is a serious request, because it involves the energies of very powerful spirits. Do this reflection when you are ready to get going and move forward in your life. If you are not, you will ignore the teachers when they make themselves known to you. You might not do this consciously, but if there is any fear or doubt about moving ahead on your spiritual journey tucked away in the back of your mind, wait until you read the entire book before doing this one. You be the judge. Just know that it will work, and work fast, so you'd better be ready and willing!

As with the other reflections, assume your most comfortable sitting position.

Now, once again, close your eyes, take three gentle breaths, and relax, allowing the relaxation to move from the top of your head, all the way down to the tip of your toes. Reflect upon the following:

Think back to your childhood. Who were the teachers who made the most positive impact upon you? From whom did you learn the most? Why? What was it about them that you felt drawn to? Was it the way they taught, their enthusiasm for the subject, or their concern for their students? If you could create the perfect spiritual teacher, what would be his or her characteristics, attributes, or special talents? Create this teacher in your mind now. See this person coming into your life to teach and mentor you on your spiritual journey. Allow this picture to form in your mind, and hold it there until it becomes comfortable. Relax and know that this person is on his or her way into your life. Give thanks.

You have just beckoned the perfect earthly teacher to come into your life. There may be many teachers and mentors in your life, some of them coming simultaneously. Be open to all of them, and know that your right intention and sincerity have attracted them, whomever they are.

Now, let us move on to your unseen teachers. The rest of this reflection calls in your angels and spirit guides.

Prepare yourself, as usual, and go into your relaxation mode.

As you breathe gently, imagine that there is a circle of God's white light surrounding you. Allow your consciousness to drift to a place within your mind. See a beautiful space in your mind's eye, a spot out in nature that is most comfortable for you. It may be by the sea, in a garden, or on a mountain top. Wherever it is, it should be special, extremely beautiful, and unique to you. Allow the image to form slowly in your mind, and help it along. Once it is formed, see yourself relaxing there, in the midst of all the beauty. As you repose there in your mind, tell yourself that you are now, beginning from this point in your life, willing to open to all of your loving helpers in Spirit. Tell them that you are ready to make contact with them, and request that your highest guidance come to you now, in a kind and loving way. Then relax and wait. You may see an image or feel a presence. Allow the image to form and the presence to remain with you, as long as you choose. When you feel you have made some kind of contact, and are satisfied, give thanks to God/Universe for this gift. Then thank the energy that joined you. Return to full consciousness, by taking a deep breath, and while exhaling, slowly open your eyes.

Record any interesting information in your journal now. Again, as before, try to write down as many details as you can, as well as your emotional responses.

This exercise has cleared your channel to the spirit realm. It has alerted your angels and guides that you are ready to work with them. It is not necessary to make voice contact at this time, or ever, to get their assistance. We each perceive them in our own way. They are helping you, even when you are unaware of them. Should you want to make even deeper contact with them, do this exercise often, once a day, and precede it with a question such as "Who is it that comes to me now? What is your name?" or "What do I need to know at this time in my life." You may or may not receive a direct answer. That depends upon your soul's growth and needs at this time, but you should be on the lookout for signs coming to you in everyday life. This is how our angels and guides communicate most often with us. And again, be aware of your own intuition. It is the voice of Spirit within.

Your Willing Heart

In reading and doing the reflection in this chapter, you have demonstrated to the Universe/God, etc., that yours is a willing heart, open to receiving your highest good. This is quite an accomplishment because it is a major step in your commitment to your soul's growth. Your teachers are waiting for you. They need you as much as you need them. From time to time, your roles will re-verse, and your teachers will become your students. Be ready for this dynamic to enter your life, and your spirit will soar.

As you seek your spiritual teachers and mentors, be aware that when you find a spiritual leader whose thoughts, words, and deeds make sense to you, make him or her your teacher. Learn as much as you can from them. When you have truly found your mentor, a bond will exist like no other. You will become one. You will feel like "family" and you will feel love and joy in their presence. Do not commit to anyone who expects you to give up all other contact with the outside world, renounce your possessions or your family, or makes you uncomfortable in any way. This is the stuff cults are made of. Study only with someone who wants you to become strong and spiritually independent. A true spiritual teacher wants also to learn, and never claims to know it all.

On your journey, align yourself with other people who share your quest and desire to grow. Keep company with those who seem to be looking for the same things. You never know. You might just find your earthly or even unearthly teachers through them, as they move through their spiritual process. You'll recognize fellow seekers by the activities they choose such as spiritual lectures, classes, or religious services. The Universe will provide you with those teachers that you need, precisely when you need them. That is the stuff of focused magic!

Affirmation 3

Affirm the following with enthusiasm, and repeat until you *believe* it:

"I open to my spiritual teachers on this Earth, and all those in Spirit. Loving angels, spirit guides, and celestial energies are ready, willing, and able to manifest into my life now. I receive them with thanks and love. As I learn and grow, I teach and expand my consciousness. And so it is!"

Nothing meaningful can be accomplished without commitment. This is especially true of our spiritual growth, one of the most challenging undertakings of our lives. While committing to a spiritual path might at first seem simple, it will require more of your focus than you might expect. Creating a magical life requires the rearrangement of life's priorities. Many of us are not sure what our priorities are. We think we know, but when we examine our life and what we hold dear, first, second, third, etc., we are often confused. In this, the fourth step on your journey, you will learn to set spiritual priorities, gain the courage to commit to the growth of your higher consciousness, focus your energy with inner work, and flow with the currents and patterns of the Universe, in order to achieve your personal sacred goals.

I have asked many of my students to state their priorities in class. I present this question, "What is the most important thing in your life?" Their answers will usually include "my children," "my job," and "my spouse." All very honest responses, but not the one

Step 4

Commit to Growth

Focus on your spiritual goals

I was listening for. After responding, I ask them to settle their focus upon the first priority in their life. I tell them to close their eyes and hold that one thought, and only that thought, for a few moments. Then I ask them to open their eyes. When the group is back from this mini-meditation, I tell them to take this priority and now put it second on their mental list. Needless to say, the confused looks abound, but I persist. "Put it second," I repeat, "and replace the top priority with God." The first response of the group is usually surprise, then a nonverbal wave of understanding overcomes the gathering.

For the spiritual seeker, the first priority, always and forever, must be God. Putting anyone or anything before Spirit will quickly scatter your energy, and it will take longer for you to accomplish your spiritual goals when you finally get around to setting them. When you really think about this, you will realize that you would have nothing without God. No home, money, spouse, children, etc. God is the Source of everything! And God always puts us first. Always. That's why God is called God.

Ins and Outs

Our tendency is to consider what is external to us as our first priority. Even our children, as wondrous a gift as they are, are still external, outside of ourselves. We unwisely rely upon the externals of life to bring us joy. We depend upon our jobs, money, friends, or family to fill the gaps in our personalities and supply the missing pieces of our emotional selves. The truth is that the only way to find lasting joy is to realize that it already exists within you. That joy, that eternal happiness, is God. God is the love within all of us that motivates us to move forward in life. Our Creator does not even require that we put God first; that is left to our own choice with the gift of free will. Spirit only makes us aware, through our successes and failures, of what works well for us and what doesn't. In my own experience and that of many of my clients and students, when God is the priority, life works better. It is that simple.

Making God our second priority is, unfortunately, one of those things we humans do naturally. Every time we are unkind to someone, withhold our love, put the chores of the day first, begrudge an offering to a church or give less money than we can actually afford to God's work, do not assist where we are needed, or abuse the Earth or animals, we are putting God second. Then we wonder why we're depressed, poor, or unsuccessful. When our focus is on the care and maintenance of others' needs, their needs become more important than our own. We are also externally focused when obtaining more money, notoriety, or possessions becomes the most important drive in our lives. In either case, we sacrifice more than we could ever know. We sacrifice true joy, peace, and a life without struggle or effort.

Shift Your Focus to the Inner You

Shifting our focus to the inner planes of our consciousness is not an easy task for us Westerners. Yet it must be a primary activity for us, if we truly want to set a spiritual course, achieve our higher goals, and stick to them. In the Eastern philosophies, people are trained from childhood to meditate as part of their daily life activities, but for us, calming down long enough to eat a sandwich is a major undertaking! That is why incorporating a daily meditation and prayer time into our schedules is very important. Daily reflection serves as a reminder to us that God is our Source and priority, and sends a message to Spirit that we are grateful for God's unconditional love and support.

In addition to calming our minds and making time for communication with God, to achieve any spiritual goals we might set we must be in flow with life. This idea of flow implies that something is already in place in the Universe that we must recognize and work with, in order to live peacefully within the scope of our personal world. There are, in fact, certain spiritual principles already working in our lives on an unseen level. They are called the Universal Laws. Living in sync with these laws can help us achieve our highest and greatest good. Following the description of each law, I have included a simple exercise section called "Stop and Focus" to assist you in understanding how you may begin working on each of them, and incorporate them into your plan of action.

The Universal Laws

Every moment of your life you are getting some help from the Universe to realize your material and spiritual goals. You might not be aware of this help because it is subtle in its effects. Scholars have determined that our lives appear to be governed by two sets of laws that hold true for all of us living on Earth. It is impossible to pinpoint the moment in time when these laws came into being, but it is believed by philosophers that they formed during the creation of the Earth and the evolution of the beings upon it. It is believed that human life is governed by natural and supernatural principles. They are called laws because they are constant, invariable, appear to be the observed regularity, and they apply to everyone, whether he or she is a believer in the law or not. The laws with which we are most familiar are the Natural Laws, or Laws of Nature. For instance, one of the Natural Laws is that the sun rises and sets during an apparent twenty-four-hour cycle in most of the observable world.

To further complicate matters, the second set of laws, the Universal (or Spiritual) Laws, govern us on the mental or unseen plane of thought. These laws work much the same as Natural Laws, but there is a marked difference in the way they are perceived. Because Natural Laws deal with the material, tangible world, we tend to accept them. You know, if you can see it, feel it, or smell it, it must be true! This down-home logic fails us when we try to apply it to the Universal Laws. We can't see the results of these laws as readily. The Natural Law of Gravity is self-evident, particularly when you get hit in the head with a brick, but the Universal Law of One is not. I think you see where I'm going with this. You're probably thinking, "The Law of What?" Let's just leave the specifics out of this for the moment, and try to grasp the whole picture.

The Spiritual or Universal Laws are harder to understand because their effects are more subtle, and sometimes take longer to manifest into our life. For instance, simplified, the Universal Law of Return states that whatever we give out, we get back. Try to tell that to someone who just put their last two dollars in the collection plate in church. The beauty of the law is that even if it takes time to work, days, months, or maybe years, it will work! That guy who gave his last dollar with loving intentions will receive back what he gave—maybe not in actual dollars, but in an opportunity to make dollars. You see? You can also see that this is why the laws of the Universe are sometimes pooh-poohed by the more linear minded among us, but whether you believe in them or not, they will still hold true for everyone.

As spiritual seekers, it is crucial to understand, as Jane L. Robertson and Deborah Hughes have explained in their book *Metaphysical Primer* (Metagnosis, 1991), that when we become aware of and work with these laws our lives become more balanced. We become physically healthier and our spiritual growth accelerates. Working with these laws entails changing our perception of the things that happen to us, from negative to positive. Our words, thoughts, and actions also need to be adjusted to reflect positive intentions. When we make every effort to work with these laws, by changing our reactions to the world, and the people and situations that come into our lives, and acting always from a place of concern for the highest good of all, we can transform our lives and tremendously expand our spiritual growth—our ultimate goal.

To clear up the mystery, what follows is a list and explanation of the Universal Laws, in simplified form. This is information that no one embarking on a spiritual journey should be without. No self-respecting metaphysician would dare admit he or she has no clue as to what these laws are, or how they impact our lives. So here they are for you. Read them and grow!

The Law of One

This law states that there is only one Source or Creator in the universe, one Deity, one God. God may be called by many names and worshipped in many ways, yet it is all one and the same energy. It follows then, that because there is only one creative energy in the Universe, this energy appears in different forms. So you could say that we: humans, animals, plants, planets, chairs, tables, cars, etc., are all expressions of this One. Therefore, we are all One. We can never be separated from the One energy. I am you, and you are me, and we are they. We are brothers and sisters to each other and all other life—seen and unseen.

This law tells us that we are always one with the One, even in our worst moments. Think about this. You are your natural parents' child, blood, genes, and all. You can never be separated from that. You will always be a part of them and they of you, no matter how you feel about each other, or what you may do in this world, good or bad. This is how God/Goddess/Spirit sees us, loving and supporting us even when we don't accept, recognize, acknowledge, worship, or become aware of God. We are still one with the One.

The other very important point of this law is that because we are all part of the same energy, what we do to or for ourselves, consequently we do to and for each other. All of the expressions of the One are affected by the individual. Therefore, what benefits you benefits me, and what hurts you hurts me. Now we may not be aware of the effect our actions may have on others, particularly those people living on the opposite side of the world, but this law tells us that in some way we are and will be affected.

It might be easier to see this connection through a practical example. When war breaks out in a foreign country, we suffer, too. We suffer compassion for the dead and their families, and on a mental/spiritual level we feel their pain. "But we're not there," you say, "How hurt can we be?" You hurt a lot when America decides to send troops into that war, and your son happens to be in the military sent over there. What if he dies? How about looking at it on a more mundane level. How angry do you get when heating oil or gasoline prices go up because our chief exporter is involved in some political action?

Sooner or later, the All is affected by the One. That's the law. So it would behoove us to act, think, speak, and affect our life and the lives of everyone on the planet in a positive way. We are mindful of this law when we are kind to each other, don't abuse our natural resources, care for our environment, and become responsible for our actions. Changing our perceptions and reactions to life's events and sorrows will also serve the world. It doesn't seem that our thoughts can have global impact, but they can and do. Think of the phrase "the ugly American," and you'll understand those global ramifications.

In short, the Law of One tells us that we are one with God, the only energy in the Universe, and that our thoughts, words, and actions affect the whole of this energy, either positively or negatively. The One Energy is the source of all life in the Universe. It is the entire Universe.

Stop and focus: To further understand the Law of One, meditate upon the thought that everything in the Universe is linked to every other thing in the Universe. Stretch your mind and use a starting point. Imagine, for example, the natural food chain, and how one animal is linked to the next in the scheme of life and growth. Now do the same with your family. Go back as far as you can, and really pay attention to your connection with your ancestors. How are you connected? What brings you together? What do you have in common? Do the same with the people with whom you work, or your close friends. Soon you will understand how very connected we all are. Now, for the ultimate test, expand this thought out of your private circle to the city you live in, the state, the country, out to foreign countries and eventually to the world. It's an amazing energy, don't you think? Try it. You'll learn something important about yourself!

The Law of Mind

Metaphysical belief is that all things are created from thought. Thought sets a vibration in motion that can literally alter the atom and manipulate matter. The Law of Mind specifically refers to the singular creative principle that formed the Universe. It is known as the Mind of God. It builds upon the Law of One, in that it further explains that this Creator is the origin of thought, and that thought shapes reality. If there is one mind, then all thought derives from the same origin, as does each individual mind. Thought expressing through vibration created the Universe.

What does this have to do with spiritual growth? The answer is that God is the pervasive energy in the Universe, which sets the forces of creation into motion by Its will, or Divine Mind. This Mind created all other minds, and all other minds share in its intelligence, because they are a part of it. Metaphysicians believe that this Divine Intelligence created all levels of our human mind such as the conscious, subconscious, and superconscious minds, and that all the energies of the Universe, are part of this grand intellect. Because of the connection to the all-powerful

God-Mind, or Universal Intelligence, our human mind can, through thought, create vibrations that can change and manipulate matter. In order to create a magical life, we must understand that we shape our lives and everything that is good or bad within them. We do this in loving cooperation with God. Positive, constructive thoughts create wealth, abundance, good health, love, and happiness. Conversely, negative, destructive thoughts create poverty, disease, sadness, and depression. God does not do negative things to us, but rather, we create them ourselves.

The Law of Mind speaks directly to the act of manifesting, or creating all that we need or want in our lives. This law, simply put, states that whatever thoughts we think work in conjunction with the Divine Mind, and what we visualize, verbalize in words, or mentally focus upon will come into being, sooner or later, as reality in our own individual world. We co-create our lives with God. You literally *are* what you think.

Spiritual healings have been effected by changing the thoughts in the mind of the sick person from those of illness to those of wellness. The chair you're sitting on was once a thought. All the matter you see around you—also thoughts. Some powerful force had to think them into being.

Stop and focus: Think about the power of your mind. Test yourself and pump this spiritual muscle. Here's how: when you are out driving today, go to a busy shopping center or mall where you generally find it difficult to get a parking space. Before you get there, relax and affirm that your space is waiting for you, very close to the entrance. Feel a wave of confidence come over you, and thank God for the space in advance. Then drive into that parking lot like the cat that swallowed the mouse, all cocky and sure of yourself. Believe. See what happens.

The Law of Duality

The Law of Duality is one of the easiest to comprehend. It simply states that everything in the Universe possesses both positive and negative energy. Everything has embodied within it male and female attributes. For instance, we know that in human biology both men and women share genetic material and characteristics of both sexes. The Chinese symbol of the yin/yang illustrates this principle. Some Western religious philosophies, mine included, believe that God is without gender, encompassing both male and female energy. God is addressed as Goddess, as in Wicca or Father/Mother God, as in my belief system, Metaphysical Science.

I have taught this law in my classes to illustrate life's natural balance. We can also understand it by examining duality from the perspective of opposites. Everything contains within itself its opposite. Inside a good and loving heart may be a few jealous feelings, or at one time or another a very smart person may say a very stupid thing. From a spiritual viewpoint, everything then has the potential to become its opposite. This is hopeful, be-cause it means that even someone who has done awful things can change. All it takes is desire and focus, and anything can become its opposite. It's a little disconcerting, but something good could also go the other way. Anyway, that's the law.

Stop and focus: The next time you are faced with a problem, rather than trying to form a solution allow your mind to see the situation from the opposite perspective. For instance, if you are having a disagreement with someone on a personal issue, such as how to invest a sum of money, let your consciousness imagine what would happen if you did the opposite of what you wanted and followed the other person's lead. Run with this and create a whole scenario, and try to do it without prejudice. Try not to make the other side look so awful, just because you don't want to do it that way. Be objective. If your counterpart does the same, you will both soon arrive at a place of compromise, effortlessly and painlessly. Try to see all things from their opposite perspective. This approach will eliminate fear of the unknown. It works.

The Law of Free Will

This is one of the most spiritual of the laws. According to the Law of Free Will, God or the Deity has given its creations the freedom of choice, without censure or judgment. This is truly the greatest gift we possess. It enables us to create the life we choose, and further proves that God is a nonjudgmental, rather than wrathful being. The Creator, by giving us this gift, has placed our destiny within our own hands, and has, in effect, agreed to support us whatever we choose. This is also the principle behind unconditional love.

Our free will can never be taken away from us. We all possess it equally. Our decisions are the building blocks of our lives, and the consequences that develop from them shape the quality of our lives. Our life is as good as the quality of the choices we make. Free will offers us the opportunity to follow any spiritual path we choose, and any religion or philosophy is fine. We also are granted the opportunity to stray from the path, or to choose to be happy or sad. Without free will we would be no more than robots, doing the bidding of a powerful Creator.

Our free will enables us to choose how we will see life. No matter what challenges we face, we have the choice to be defeated or energized by the outcomes. Our spiritual growth depends upon making wise choices that enrich our soul, and move us closer to our enlightenment.

The freedom to choose how to perceive life enables us to move forward past pain, grief, trauma, and lack. It is a precious, precious gift.

Stop and focus: This one is easy. Rather than using just your logic to make choices and decisions, try allowing your gut feelings to lead the way. This is a commitment you can make to your Spirit, by relying on it to guide your path as you determine your spiritual goals. We all know this to be our intuitive self at work, but do we really allow it to assist us in making really important life choices? Don't worry. Your free will is still in play here. The difference is that when you let your higher self speak to you, and you actually listen to it, you express your free will from a deep place of wisdom, a place of God within you, so you can't ever make the wrong choice. Of course you can ignore it, which is your right, having free will.

The Law of Attraction

This law tells us that the way we think attracts certain people, situations, events, and problems to us. According to the Law of Attraction, our thoughts, our conscious and subconscious minds, have the power to draw particular energy into our lives. These energies manifest themselves as positive or negative people or situations in our individual world. The effects can be joyful or upsetting.

A good way to understand this law is to remember the phrase "Like attracts like." Positive energy attracts positive energy, and negative energy attracts negative energy. If you think positive thoughts, and act in positive harmonious ways, that is what will fill your life. Acting and thinking negatively sends a vibration from your conscious and subconscious mind, which moves matter, and materializes more for you to be negative about! The Universe will give you back what you put into it. Therefore, it is very important for a spiritual person to think and perform in positive ways, in order to live a joyful life.

Look at your friends. What type of people do you attract? Are they positive or negative thinkers? Are they loving and supportive, or irresponsible and self-centered? The people you attract are mirrors of yourself. Examining your closest, most important relationships will tell you whether you are a positive or negative person.

I'm sure you have heard the phrase "Money goes to money." That's correct. It does, because money, or prosperity and abundance energy, attracts itself. The way to attract money, if you have none, is to start thinking that you already do! Tell yourself your money is on its way to you, and stop giving lip service to lack. Talking about lack is the perfect way to stay poor!

Many of my clients have relationship and money problems. One client in particular cannot understand why she keeps attracting friends who are self-centered, competitive, and irresponsible with money. She doesn't want to accept that she is the same way, therefore that is what she is attracting. When she changes her thoughts she will change what she attracts.

Working well with the Law of Attraction requires that we pay attention to our lives, the people around us, and our problems, take responsibility for them, and commit to changing our thoughts and the way we do things. Replacing old, outmoded thinking and making minor personality and attitude adjustments can literally turn a stressful life into a magical one.

Stop and focus: Here's a focus for you. Take a look in the mirror. Yep, a real mirror. What do you see? Yeah, I'm sure you're gorgeous, but beyond that, do you see a happy face, a confident face, a loving face, or a depressed face, an insecure face, or an angry face? News flash—what you see is what you get! Think about that when you want to attract something into your life.

The Law of Plenty

Simply put, the Law of Plenty expresses that the Universe is abundant with everything that anyone could ever need or want, and there's plenty for all of us. To tap into the richness and abundance of the Universe, we need only accept and declare that God is the Source of all good in our life. This sends a message of sincere gratitude to the Creator, which in turn is rewarded with opportunities and advantages to succeed in the material world. Fear is removed and our heart opens to receive the very best the Universe has to offer us on the emotional, mental, and spiritual levels.

Stop and focus: Ask yourself, "Do I truly believe that I can have all that I want, and so can everyone else, because the Universe is rich and abundant and available to me?" "Do I truly believe that God is the source of all material and spiritual good in my life?" Answer these questions honestly. No one is watching and there won't be a quiz on them. If the answer is a truly honest "yes," then you are focusing your soul in a constructive direction. If not, take some time to reflect on why you don't believe. You'll be surprised at yourself.

The Law of Return

This law complements the previous one, making us aware of the way plenty remains constant in our lives. The Law of Return is sometimes known as the Law of Circulation, or the Law of Giving and Receiving. It basically states that what you give, you receive. What you give may be time, energy, kindness, love, anger, hate, prejudice, money, etc. Whatever you give you get back, and the spiritual belief is that you get it back in spades! Some religions say you get it back ten-fold, and still others, one-hundred-fold! That's both a comforting and frightening thought. You would think that this law presents an easily under-standable lesson, but it is one of the most difficult for people to learn—especially where money is concerned.

Let's talk about that for a moment. If a person truly believes that he will get back what he gives to charity, let's say, then he should have no problem donating 10 percent of what he earns to God's work. That makes perfect sense to me, because I know that God is the source of the money anyway, and God's source is limitless. So what's the big deal? The big deal is greed and fear. It astounds me that we can plunk down $8.00 a week to see a movie, plus $5.00 for popcorn, and yet have a problem con-tributing even $5.00 to a church. What most people don't get is that the $13.00 you "contributed" to the propri-etor of the movie theater is not coming back to you. The $5.00 you gave to God's work will—ten-fold and one-hun-dred-fold! What makes more sense to you?

The Law of Return is also called the Law of Giving and Receiving. It is the intention with which you give that opens your channel to receive. So, even if you give a lot of money to God's work, you may not get it back if you give it with hesitation, anger, or fear. This law teaches us that the spirit behind the giving is what makes it work. When we give with a generous and loving heart, with positive intentions, without expecting or demanding a return, we are well rewarded by the Universe for our generosity. Spiritually speaking, we must give to say thank you to God for all that we have. We must also give with the desire to help others and share our blessings. You might call it unconditional giving. Once you give, you must detach from the result, meaning that you do not focus upon how what you have given is used, or require that it be used in a particular way, or care about when or how it will come back to you. That act of total release tells the Universe that you are ready to receive.

Stop and focus: How hard is this? You've got to give to get. Period. Yet this is one of the most difficult laws to implement in life, because fear of lack is often greater than love. Sad, isn't it? How do you see it? Can you give to your Source a small portion of what it gives you, without hesitation or expectation? Focus on that for a while.

The Law of Permanence and Nonpermanence

This law states that the only thing permanent in the Universe is God. Everything else is temporary. Everything. Negativity, bad times, poverty, ill health—all are temporary. This is hopeful because it makes it clear that our problems are not permanent fixtures in our lives. Accepting joy is easier when you realize that everything will pass, instead of focusing on the difficult situations and expecting that they will never go away. We must focus on the joyful and expect it, too. It is also important to keep in mind that the good stuff is also temporary. This is not to say that you should always wait for the worst to happen when you have experienced a time of joy and prosperity. I know how easy it is for us to think that things are too good to be true, and that sooner or later something bad will happen. Not true. In accepting that good things are temporary, we are simply remaining detached from them. We must realize that if we lose all our money, become ill, our sweetheart leaves us, or whatever, that we will survive and recreate our lives again, because we have the power to make good things happen. When you look at life this way, you remain in flow with your life's spiritual plan, handling the good with the bad, and letting neither distort your perception of life, or create fear.

Stop and focus: The focused spiritual seeker should have no trouble getting the gist of this law. Ask yourself, "Would I be okay and stay happy if I lost all that I had tomorrow?" You can never lose God. God is love, and love is all you need.

The Law of Reincarnation

This law, and the Law of Karma to follow, are often called the Twin Laws because they work hand-in-hand. Two-thirds of the world's religions believe in reincarnation. The basic premise of this spiritual law is that the human soul lives many lives. It comes to Earth through physical birth, in order to experience life, learn lessons, make contributions to others, and to serve God. As the soul lives in the current body, it plays out its present role, as male or female, resolves past-life issues (old karma) that it has brought into this life, and creates new ones (new karma). When the physical body dies, the soul has the choice to remain in spirit form or return to Earth in another body, to complete and resolve any remaining karma. As this cycle repeats itself, the soul spiritually advances and expands, and moves closer to God or enlightenment.

When your soul decided to come to Earth, you were given the free will to choose your time of birth, gender, parents, genetics, race, lessons to be learned, etc. Every aspect was your choice, which implies that you are totally responsible for your fate. Not God. You. Responsibility is one of the greatest teachings of this law.

Stop and focus: Do you take responsibility for all you think, say and do? Or, do you have a tendency to blame others and God for all that happens to you? If your response is "yes" toward the latter of these two questions, you are obviously working against the Universe, since this Law of Reincarnation tells us that we ultimately chose our own destiny.

The Law of Karma

Another name for this law is the Law of Cause and Effect. This law should be viewed as a cycle, a process of ongoing learning. Whatever we put into the Universe or cause to happen, in the form of action, word, and thought, produces a result or effect. We can never stop thinking, acting, or communicating; therefore we are continually creating karma. *Karma* in the ancient Sanskrit language literally means "act, word, or deed." Whatever we do has repercussions. That is that. Whatever you create will have an effect on someone or something, which will eventually get back to you, either in this life or the next. That is why it is important to create positivity and joy, rather than negativity and pain. Karma may be carried over from one life to the next, until all of our karma is resolved. (It is believed that the masters such as Jesus and the Buddha do not need to return to Earth, having resolved all of their karma.) Then the soul becomes a master teacher, with the choice to come back to Earth, not to resolve karma, but to teach the rest of us how to grow spiritually.

Some think that karma is a sort of debt we have to pay back for being bad in another lifetime. It is not. I prefer to think of it as karmic resolution, or a way for our soul to complete the learning of lessons we have not previously understood. Karma can be good, too. This is easily seen in the good things that happen. I tell my clients that if things are going well in their lives, they must have done something good in previous lifetimes, because they are reaping the rewards of creating a magical life well lived.
Stop and focus: The spiritual warrior needs to be aware without a doubt that one of the reasons he or she is here on the planet is to learn lessons and to resolve issues. *This should be a major focus for you.* Think about the lessons you've already learned and be very careful of your words, thoughts, and actions from now on, because they carry great and mighty implications for your soul and its growth.

The Law of Love

This is probably the most powerful and greatest of the Universal Laws. The Law of Love states that all beings and all things are loved unconditionally. Every energy in the

Universe is loved and accepted by the Creator, the Source of the energy, or God. God is often referred to as a Being of Light and Love, which gives equally and unconditionally of Itself to all of Its creations. This reference to love is not the gooey or romantic type, but rather, this love is more of a fact. It is less emotional in its nature, and may be understood as total acceptance and contentment. God accepts everything in the universe, even us, with all of our faults, along with everything in the Universe, enabling us to create life as we choose, without judgment, and with full divine support.

The Law of Love also speaks to the love of self, or self-love. It seems corny to me when I hear people speak of the need to love yourself. I used to respond, "So what does that mean?" Through my understanding of this law, I have realized that it means accepting myself, with all of my faults, talents, physical attributes, and mental perceptions, without self-condemnation, or self-hatred. We have been given, by our Creator, the perfect mind, body, and spirit to complete the mission we have set forth for ourselves on this planet. When we comprehend that, we will love ourselves unconditionally, and accept with contentment all of the things we are, and this love will radiate from us as a kind of light energy. Imagine the miraculous outpouring of light if we all felt this way about ourselves. How great is that?

Stop and focus: Do you know what unconditional love feels like? If so, you are blessed. If not, you're not paying attention. This kind of love is all around you because God is all around you. Focus on becoming aware of love in action, every day of your life.

At this point, I am sure you can see how understanding the Universal Laws and living in harmony with them will greatly increase the likelihood of reaching our spiritual goals successfully, whatever they may be. Now it is time to get to the setting of those goals that are crucial to living and creating your magical life.

Setting the Stage: Creating Spiritual Goals

I spent many years as an actress and director in the theater. The process of designing and building a stage set was always a source of wonder and amazement to me. As a director, I loved working with set designers to create the backdrop upon which the play would be performed. Slowly, meticulously, and gently, walls would come to life, rooms would form, gardens would blossom, rivers would flow, all in the relatively small confines of a theater stage. As an actor, the play always seemed to come to life to me once I got to work on the set. Most of the theater rehearsals are held elsewhere, away from the stage proper, usually in a barren room with a few chairs set up to represent set pieces, the floor having been drawn off with masking tape to simulate the dimensions of the actual stage. This is done so that the set can be built without actors in the way of the process. When finally the actors and director are let loose to do their thing on the stage, costumes, lights, props, makeup, and music are added to complete and enhance the experience. Then the true magic of the theater begins to happen.

When you set your spiritual goals you set the stage for your growth. You prepare the environment of your life for your spiritual *performance*. Of course, your spiritual journey will last much longer than the duration of a play, but pulling together all of the elements of your life to create a magical future requires the same concentration and dedication, except that it is forever. Don't be afraid of that. You are making your spiritual commitment to your soul, to forever live in love, joy, and peace. Now that's not so bad, is it?

"What are spiritual goals, anyway?" you say. They are the specific ends toward which our individual spiritual efforts are directed. They are the results for which we strive. These results are different for each of us because the needs of our souls are unique to each individual. When we were in spirit-form, directly conversing with God, if you will, we decided to come back to Earth and live a lifetime learning and growing our physical and spiritual selves. We chose the circumstances of our birth and lives to help us reach these goals. Other souls agreed to work with us, because we had similar goals, or they were willing to help us achieve ours. Our soul's spiritual goals are directly related to the lessons that we incarnated to learn. In learning these lessons we expand our consciousness and grow more enlightened, or closer to God.

There you have it. Now your task is to figure out what your lessons might be and then set your goals accordingly. Realistically speaking, understanding these goals could take a lifetime, so we can only set them as we realize them. Your list will change and shift over the years. As you reach one goal, another might emerge. This growth is a process, which means it is ongoing. We are works in progress, and our Spirit is always changing, learning, growing, and expanding.

Since realizing your goals is quite a task, even for the experienced seeker, I have fashioned a list of them for you. Remember that they are ends, not means. They are what we are striving for. In chapter 5 we'll talk about what to do to reach these goals. Look the list over and allow your intuition to tell you what is right for you. If you do not see all of your goals here, feel free to add some. It would be impossible to list the millions of individual goals, so by all means, write your own. Choose one goal to achieve at a time. You may make a list in your spiritual journal of all the goals that seem right for you, and then work on them one-by-one, until you have integrated them into your life.

Your spiritual goals toward creating a magical life might be:

- To have a loving relationship with God.

- To value and love yourself.

- To value life on all levels of existence.

- To harm none.

- To live a peaceful, harmonious, joyful, and loving life.

- To receive abundance and prosperity into your life, release fear and thoughts of lack, and significantly increase and improve your finances.

- To release struggle and effort from your life.

- To accept yourself as you are, without self-criticism and self-hatred, loving your faults as well as your attributes.

- To develop self-esteem and self-confidence.

- To give up anger, from the past or present.

- To release fear.

- To forgive.

- To believe in yourself as lovable, receive love joyfully, and give love freely to others.

- To give up ill health and accept perfect health.

- To eliminate prejudice and judgment from your consciousness.

- To learn to love unconditionally.

- To trust in yourself and your decisions.

- To believe that you deserve the best.

- To accept and use your talents, and/or to use them to make life better for yourself and others.

- To accept success in whatever endeavor you choose, and to release all thoughts of failure.

- To make a contribution to the world in your own unique way.

- To release oversensitivity to other's words or treatment, and emotional overreactions.

- To accept and have faith in your intelligence.

- To extend to and become spiritually and emotionally closer to other people.

- To protect and nurture animals.

- To protect and nurture the Earth and the environment.

- To open to sharing your life with someone you love.

- To overcome loneliness.

- To overcome depression.
- To allow yourself to be emotionally intimate with someone you trust.
- To seek out and discover your heart's desires and live them!

Here is a quick reference spiritual goal list:
I am here to learn about:

- Patience
- Trust
- Loyalty
- Faith
- Abuse
- Violence
- Death
- Abandonment
- Poverty
- Wealth
- Sex
- Health

As with the other, this quick reference list can go on and on, because there are as many lessons to learn as there are people on the planet! Add yours.

Reflection 4

Hitting the Mark!

If you are still confused as to what your spiritual goals might be, this reflection will help. Go into it with an open mind, without expectation, and let your higher self, the part of you that is very wise, tell your consciousness what it needs to know.

As with the other reflections, assume your comfortable sitting position.

Now, once again, close your eyes, take three gentle breaths, and relax, allowing the relaxation to move from the top of your head, all the way down to the tips of your toes. Reflect upon the following:

> *Think about how you perceive your life. Do you see it as generally positive or negative? Happy or sad? Objectively observe the quality of your life, right here, right now. Focus on the areas of your life that you feel need improvement. Tell yourself why you feel these areas need to improve. Now, in order to create your spiritual goals, say the following statement to yourself, and allow your higher self to fill in the ending: "My life would be so much happier and more fulfilled if I committed to working on _____." When you are content with the answer, give thanks to God/Universe for this gift of personal discovery. Then take a deep breath, and while exhaling, return to full consciousness, and slowly open your eyes.*

Record any interesting information in your journal now. Again, as before, try to write down

**as many details as you can, as well as your
emotional responses.**

You may repeat this reflection as needed, setting one spiritual goal at a time. You should reflect a profile of who you are and the way you are presently responding to the events that have occurred in your life, up to this moment in time. They should seem like welcome solutions to you, a relief from the stress under which you have been living. When you work diligently and joyfully toward fulfilling your goals, you will be well on your way to creating your magical life!

Take Time

Now that you understand how to set spiritual goals for your life, you will need to commit to working with the very powerful Laws of the Universe, as you focus on reaching them. As you have seen, we work with these laws in a very fundamental way, through prayer and meditation. It is crucial for everyone in search of a spiritual way of life to take time to meditate, pray, and reflect. This act is a precious, nurturing, and life-enriching gift you give to yourself. A few moments in silent meditation can mean the difference between reaching your goals sooner, or living in chaos and turmoil a bit longer. I favor a morning meditation because it sets the mood for my whole day. I review the goals I have set for myself, enlist God's help, and relax in the joy of knowing that all is well. My prayers are always in the form of affirmations, just like the ones that end each of these chapters. You can craft your own to suit your goals, or simply have a dialogue with God. Tell Spirit that you have chosen to make your relationship with God your highest priority in your life. When you do, the answers to all of life's problems and questions will become very clear. You will find that living in harmony with the Universal Laws is just as uncomplicated as with the Natural Laws, and your spirit will swell with joy, wisdom, and contentment with each moment spent in quiet reflection, as you see this magic taking form in your physical world

Affirmation 4

Affirm the following with enthusiasm, and repeat until you *believe* it:

"Focusing on my spiritual goals is a joyful act for me. I pray and meditate each day. I am fully aware of my thoughts, words, and actions, and direct them in positive, life-enriching ways. I accept and commit to working toward my spiritual goals, in harmony with the Universal Laws, to change my life for the better. And so it is!"

You may read, study, research, and devour all the material you can on the subject of spirituality, but none of it will make any impact on your life until you do something about it. You must not only decide to live a life that is full of joy and wonder, you must actually practice those principles every day. When we have decided to live magically, we have chosen to rely on ourselves and our Spirit to create a wondrous life on Earth. To do that we must apply these concepts to our daily activities. Over time, making this application becomes easier and easier until it is second nature to you. This step in your spiritual evolution will teach you how to successfully empower your life and forever reap the rewards of your efforts by releasing fear and developing your intuition, the magical creative power within you.

Step 5

Live Magically

Create an enchanted life

Intuition: The Voice of Wisdom

Your God-given innate gift of intuition is your key to living a fulfilling life. This is the little voice inside you that tells you when it feels right to do something. This is also the nagging feeling you get when you just know that you shouldn't have eaten that last taco, because it would keep you up all night. Or, it's that voice in your head that you hear saying, "Don't let your friend persuade you to buy this dress. You know chartreuse is not your color!" Yet, we eat that taco and buy that unflattering dress. Why? Because we don't know how to recognize when God is speaking to us. We think it's just our own logic talking, but I can tell you that Spirit speaks to us in many, many ways, both profound and mundane. The simple decisions require the most help because we are called upon to make so many of them in a single day. Just think about it. How many decisions have you already made today? I'll bet there were plenty, even though you might not put much energy into making them.

This morning you had to decide to get up out of bed. You had to decide to take a shower, have a cup of coffee, water the plants, open the shades, etc. These are all decisions, and they are relentless. The more important they are, the more we notice them. When you are deciding to get married or divorced, to have a baby, or change careers, you pay more attention to the decision-making process, but your Spirit doesn't help you more with the tough decisions than the easy ones, because It doesn't judge anything. To God, the lowly mouse is as important as the mighty human. All are one. Therefore, God will be most willing to help you make any and all decisions, from what to have for dinner, to giving up an addiction. This "Voice of God," as I call our intuition, speaks to us every moment of our lives. The trouble is, we don't always hear it, nor do we always heed it. "But how do I recognize this voice?" you say. "How do I know the difference between it and my own mind?" "It just sounds like me. Isn't it just me?" I'm glad you asked.

Now You See It, Now You Don't

The above questions are the ones I hear most often from my own clients and students. Many of us have trouble distinguishing between the prompting of our intuition and our logical mind. Sometimes we are very conscious of the fact that we are receiving a message, and sometimes we are not. There really is a difference. All it takes is a heightened awareness. You must be willing to open to the subtle messages of the universe. Your intuition will demonstrate itself through your gut reactions, dreams, or a sense of *knowing*. Some people actually *hear* words in the mind's ear. There are many ways in which our intuition makes itself known to us.

You might think that your gut reactions are simply first impressions. For example, you meet someone and instantly like or dislike him or her. You think that this is your gut reaction to the individual, but it is really an emotional response to some karmic connection you have with this person. Somewhere in time you have met, and are meeting again in this lifetime. but your intuitive gut reaction is not an emotional response. It is a general feeling that something is right or not right about a situation, depending upon the comfort level you are experiencing at the moment. You must ask yourself that if you were to take all the emotion out of the event, and react as an observer, would the situation then be comfortable or uncomfortable? Your intuition is speaking to you through this comfort level. It is neutral and emotionless. It will convey to you a feeling of peace or uneasiness. Many people experience an actual physical response in the stomach area when their intuition is communicating with them. If the message is positive, the physical feeling will be one of relaxation. If it is negative, the feeling will be of tightness.

The reactions to intuition working through us are universal. We all experience them at some time or another in our lives. When you learn to tap into this helpful ability, you will call upon it to demonstrate itself more and more often, because it is always right!

Start Listening—Now!

I'm sure there have been times when you have somehow "known" when something was good for you or not, and yet you have chosen to ignore that message, only to find that you did yourself more harm than good by not following that calling in the first place. Other people will have a strong influence upon whether we listen to our intuition or not. You might ignore what you "know" is right for you in order to do something for someone else. Even though you are motivated by the right intentions you could suffer, because when you act on anything it should be in the highest and greatest good of all those concerned, including yourself.

Our intuition also makes itself know to us in more subtle ways. For instance, you are having a conversation with a friend who needs your counsel. He or she is in the throes of a life-changing decision and wants your help. As you are chatting, you make a statement that is so profound the Buddha himself might have made it. You are more startled by what came out of your mouth than your friend. You might think, "Did I say that?" Well, no.

Rather, yes. Or, yes and no. You actually spoke the words, but your higher, intuitive self—your intuition—spoke from your superconscious mind. All the profound knowledge you need is stored there, because it is the part of our mind that is directly connected to God. You don't recognize it, because the phrase you uttered is so remotely foreign to anything you might normally say, but your God-self would say it. That's your intuition speaking directly through you. If you are not very sensitive to the voice of your intuition, you are not alone. People who are very psychic or naturally intuitive don't seem to have any trouble with this, although most of the rest of us do. There are ways that you can become more aware of these subtle vibrations, but, just like anything else, you have to commit to developing your sensitivity.

Tweaking Your Instrument

This intuitive sense that we possess can be further honed and enhanced by working on a few principles. To truly live magically, you must be willing to make magic. Magic exists in the realm of the unseen. It depends upon trust and faith. That's what it will take to follow your intuitive messages, because it will require effort to discern them. Here is an easy exercise you can do to help you to recognize and flex your intuitive muscle.

> *Close your eyes for a moment, and breathe slowly and evenly. As you breathe, relax and be gently aware of your stomach. Ask your higher self, your intuitive self, to give you a sensation in your stomach, which is not painful, that will indicate a "yes" answer for you when you need a quick solution to a problem. Wait a moment*

and focus on this area of your body. What sensation do
you feel? It could be a simple contraction or flutter. It is
different for everyone, so record this sensation in your
mind and trust it to be a message from your higher con-
sciousness in guiding your decisions. Do the same thing
for a "no" answer, or you can simply know that if you
get no response in your stomach area when you ask a
question, the answer is no. It's up to you, and this does
work! Try your best to trust it. Start out by using it to
make simple decisions. As you get more confident, use it
for more intense decisions.

You can also develop your sensitivity by becoming more aware of your surroundings as you move through life every day. Pay attention to the way you feel when you walk into a room. Are you comfortable or not? When it comes to people, don't ignore your perceptions about someone when you first meet him or her. Without being rude to the person, you can assess your level of comfort around him or her. I am not talking about emotion here. I'm simply stating that you need to put your own ego aside, whether or not you are intimidated by this person's accomplishments or demeanor, and allow your higher self to make the call. If you are intimidated, but are intrigued by the person anyway, your intuition is probably telling you that it would be fine to get to know this person. If you are intimidated and you are not comfortable with them, the opposite is true.

Each day you will be given messages. Look around you for signs from the Universe. One of my students has successfully tapped into her intuitive self by paying attention to details. She was searching for a new career, having been disenchanted with the one she had pursued for many years. Feng Shui, the ancient Chinese art of furniture placement and energy flow, was very interesting to her. This art deals with the grouping of furniture in auspicious arrangements to enhance the good fortune, good health, and general well-being of a home's inhabitants. As she studied this subject, she had a strong intuitive feeling that she should be working with children. This seemed to be in conflict with Feng Shui, because she didn't see specifically how it applied to children, other than the general benefits they would reap from living in a home that had been treated. Upon further study, she learned that this discipline also included the design and construction of buildings. Bingo! The light went off in her consciousness and she realized what her intuition was trying to tell her. She would pursue the design of school buildings and use Feng Shui techniques in the design and placement of student classrooms, desks, etc.! This is a relatively untouched field, and she was excited to pursue it. If that were not enough, she received a letter in the mail seeking volunteers for an advisory committee of local citizens in her town. The object of the committee was to research and advise officials as to the construction of new school buildings! This sign was too obvious to be ignored. She quickly made arrangements to attend a meeting of the committee and volunteer her services. She recognized the opportunity to serve the children of her community and her eternal soul. When we are in tune with our intuition and in flow with our Spirit the results are amazing! Yet, there is more.

Use It, Don't Lose It

It is simply not enough to recognize our intuition working in our lives. Once we do, we have an obligation to follow it. My student mentioned above could have easily
ignored even those very clear signs, if she chose. God has
given us the free will to take or leave divine advice—all in a
day's lessons, I'm afraid. When we chose not to follow the
prompting of our heart we simply take another path. The
road to our magical life takes a turn for the worse. It will
simply take longer to reach our goals. Following these
messages will put us on the spiritual track and keep us
there. It is a known fact that the fastest way to get from
point A to point B is a straight line. Why take the road
with all the curves and bends? Listening to your intuition
will lead you down the right path, but you still must take
the first step. Don't forget the stomach exercise in the
previous section. It is a very useful tool in a pinch!

When you are clear on what you are being led to do,
then do it! Take action. If you do not, you have most definitely told Spirit, "Thanks, but no thanks." Just listening
will not do you any good. You must couple word with
action. Then you will, in effect, be waving your magic
wand at the world and making dreams come true. There
is a world of difference between listening to your intuition and *following* it. Doing the latter is proof of our commitment to our personal joy and enlightenment.

Here is a word of caution: once you have waved your
magic wand, do not entertain any doubts. Even if you feel
you have followed your intuition and the situation has
not worked out the way you hoped, you have not made a
mistake. Only Spirit knows the whole picture. You only
see the situation unfolding before you step by step. This is

a concept I made clear to my student who was following her messages. I counseled her about remaining unattached to the results of the action. We need not worry so much about how we want something to work out, but rather, we must have faith in the process of life.

My student wanted to work on Feng Shui principles in her school system, and ultimately, to have an impact on the design and construction of the new buildings. I told her that she might not get that far, but that if God was intuitively prompting her to pursue this, that she would have an impact on someone or something in some way. I proposed a possible outcome, that she might be laughed out of the meeting for offering concepts way outside the mainstream of her community. Then I advised her to accept whatever the result because she was meant to be there. Someone sitting in the room might be affected positively by her presentation and moved to make a change in his own life, and she might never know it. Always trust that your intuition is leading you toward the path of the greatest growth for your soul, and possibly that of others who cross that path, whatever the result!

Another student described a situation that was difficult for him. At one time he was working for a rather unscrupulous boss who had done some illegal maneuvering in the workplace—enough to get him arrested. This student knew his boss' actions and was deeply disturbed by them. When the case came to trial several employees were asked to write letters to the officiating judge on behalf of his boss' character. My student wrote one, not condoning or defending his boss, but rather asking the judge to consider forgiveness. This was a very commendable thing to do, yet he was bothered by having to write the letter at all because he just knew he shouldn't. After serving jail time, his boss was back on the job doing the same shady things he had done before. The student was angry with him. I told the student that he shouldn't bear any resentment, because he had the choice to write the letter or not, and he chose to do it, even though his intuition told him not to. The reason why he was feeling angry was because he compromised himself and his values to do it. It was obvious that the boss didn't care one way or the other. When you ignore your messages you pay the price. My student thought he was acting in everyone's highest good by writing an honest letter. He did act in everyone's highest good except his own. He is still upset about the whole thing. Sometimes ignoring God can be really uncomfortable!

The Magic Touch

You have the magic touch. Accept that. You have the power to create something from nothing. We all do. It is our spiritual obligation to our eternal soul to create joy, love, harmony, abundance, and peace. This is the making of an enchanted life. How do we do that? First we listen and act on the messages from Spirit coming to us through our intuition. Then we get out of our own way by not overanalyzing, fretting, and worrying every situation to death! Creating a magical life requires us to stop thinking and start responding, without resistance, to the flow of our deepest desires as they make themselves known to us. This resistance is our logical mind. It is more than willing to tell us that we are crazy to follow our intuition, because it makes no sense. Sometimes, following your messages *will* seem crazy and make no sense, but again, faith is the key. We have to break the habit of going into our logical mind, particularly in situations where logic does not apply. Living magically means taking chances, relying on that sense of inner knowing to make decisions. That is not to say that you should never make another logical decision as long as you live, but rather you should allow your intuition to work along with your logical mind to craft the most desirable life for yourself.

Courage! Release Your Fear

"Who put the 'ape' in 'apricot?' Courage. Whadda' they got that I ain't got? Courage!" The words of the Cowardly Lion in *The Wizard of Oz* have always been very special to me. They represent overcoming fear, and becoming the person of strength that we know ourselves to be. The Lion looked fierce and strong, but inside was wracked with fears. His inner and outer personas were in direct conflict with one another. Are yours?

When you ignore your intuitive self, you most often do so out of fear. When I suggested this to my student, who wrote the letter for his boss, he immediately said that he wasn't afraid of anything. I said that he might not have realized that he was fearful, and I suggested that he might have written the letter because he wanted to keep his job, and was concerned about the possible repercussions if he didn't. I also added that he might have been afraid of the opinions of his coworkers had he been the only one not to comply. When he thought about this, he agreed that there was some anxiety involved.

Fear is the greatest deterrent to joy. It can and does stop us dead from creating magic. Humans are afraid of lots of things. If I tried to list them all I would be at this

computer forever. What are your fears? If you have trouble answering that question (or maybe facing it), here is a
quick fear-releasing exercise for you. We'll take this exercise to a higher level in the reflection at the end of the
chapter, but for now, it can't hurt to begin releasing those
pent-up and potentially destructive emotions:

> *When you are in doubt as to whether or not to follow
> your intuition, you must ask yourself this very impor-
> tant question, "What am I afraid of?" Really focus on
> this. Let yourself dig deeply into those fears that seem to
> come to the surface when you ask the question. Don't
> second-guess yourself. Simply allow your first reaction to
> the question to come forward. Then take an objective
> look at it. Is the fear that surfaces valid, or in the
> scheme of your life, is it really that important to your
> happiness? You might find that most of your misgivings
> are simply outmoded ways of looking at your life—the
> old you versus the new you. Do you still think the old
> way, or are you ready to throw off old modes of being for
> an enlightened future? Face the fear and let it go.
> Release its control over you, because you no longer need
> it. Breathe and relax. It is done.*

This exercise could be painful, but it is absolutely necessary for your growth. Recognizing your fears, address-
ing them head-on, and releasing them, gets you through
that impasse and catapults you into a new way of life.
Getting past his own fear and doubt is the most difficult,
and most rewarding experience a human can have, second
only to that of giving and receiving unconditional love.

It takes unbridled courage to live a magical life. The
spiritual path is not for the faint of heart! Courage equals

faith. Rely on your inner knowing and you will live the most joyful of life experiences because you will be in harmony with your values. Having courage, while difficult to muster, helps you sleep nights. You know you have done what is right and perfect for all those concerned, including yourself. In this way, you cannot go wrong.

Have the courage to call upon your intuition in making simple decisions. Use it to help you decide where to eat, park, play, how to spend money, what classes to take, which route to drive to work, what vacation to go on, or even what furniture to buy. Employ your inner sense to every situation and it will not fail you. If you are brave enough to try this with simple choices, you are flexing the muscle and building your strength so that you can trust it when the really tough decisions come along. It won't fail you there, either. When major life decisions have to be made, your intuitive sense will be the guiding force of love/God acting in your life.

This Magic Moment: Make It Last With Practical Action

We are fortunate to be living in the age of enlightenment. This movement toward a consciousness of the Spirit is growing and thriving in our society. You have become a vital part of it simply through reading this book. To participate fully in this magical moment in time, the spiritual seeker will be called upon to accept his psychic/intuitive nature and be ready to develop those abilities. To do so you must simply have the willing intention. This sends a vibration to the Universe that you are open to learn about and receive the benefits of an expanded awareness.

There are practical things you can do to create and live this magical existence. To be a modern-day mystic you must put more faith in things that cannot be seen or touched, and in your natural responses. You must be ready to awaken to your Spirit. This means that you allow yourself to pay more attention to what is intuitive than to what is logical. You must be brave enough to undertake this commitment to yourself knowing that you will be going against the mainstream. Most people will not explore such a lifestyle because it is much easier to live in a world where spirituality is reserved for Sunday rather than living it each day. To come out as a spiritual person is not as carefree as it may seem. It takes a newfound courage. Others may not understand because they are not yet on the same level of growth as you are. Not everyone is brave enough to take that step, to break away from the norm. Therefore, you should not expect them to. Each person's growth is meant to take its own path, and its own time. Each of us will come to our greatness in our own way. Accept people at their own psychic/intuitive/ spiritual level. They may be in your life because they need to learn from you, and you from them. We are not all meant to be the same. The differences among us are intentional. The Creator allows us to learn all that we choose to learn, intellectually or spiritually, in our own way. Give up your expectations and people will not disappoint you and you will not disappoint yourself.

Traditionally, organized religion has created expectations. Metaphysicians believe that such expectations limit spiritual growth. Telling people that there is a right way and a wrong way to live inhibits their choices. That is not to say that we should live a life of self-indulgence and disregard for others, it simply means that we must decide for ourselves to live in harmony with the world, harming no one or nothing, and respecting all life. That is the spiritual and magical way of life.

To further take advantage of this magical moment in time, the spiritual seeker must establish a relationship with God/Goddess/Creator/Universe that they express daily. The practice of prayer and meditation eliminates fear and keeps us in constant contact with what is truly important in life. God will never leave you. All God asks is that you remind yourself of your greatness, your birthright, and live in that grace.

I have too often heard angry complaints from my clients about how God has deserted them in their time of need. They have said that they felt that God has left their life and that they are alone. This is impossible. God cannot, nor will not leave you. You are God, God is you, one and the same. When our faith is tested is the time when God is closest to us. We are the ones who abandon God, not the other way around. If things don't work out as we want them to, we blame God for it. That is how we close the door on our Spirit. Instead of realizing that trying times are just lessons and reminders that we live in a material world that is not perfect, and that it is our job to return to our spiritual nature at that very moment, we simply reject God. It's easier than taking responsibility for our lessons. There is never a time when God will leave you. Don't leave God.

Reflection 5

Opening to Spirit

Taking the leap of faith that is required of a spiritual pioneer can be a fear-producing experience, because in doing so you tell the Universe that you are hereby accepting full responsibility for every aspect of your being—body, mind, and spirit. This reflection is designed to help you open to this aspect of yourself, gently and without fear. Embrace this commitment and enjoy your life!

As with the other reflections, assume your comfortable sitting position.

Now, once again, close your eyes, take three gentle breaths, and relax, allowing the relaxation to move from the top of your head all the way down to the tips of your toes. Reflect on the following:

As you breathe gently, allow all of your fears to release from your consciousness by telling them to go. You may feel a tightness in your stomach as you do this. Relax with that feeling until it subsides. When the feeling is gone, tell yourself that you are ready to move forward on your spiritual path, invite God/Spirit/Universe into your life, and give thanks for the opportunities for growth that await you on your journey. Silently make a commitment to allow your intuitive self to guide you in making choices and decisions. Put your confidence in it. Relax with this idea for a few moments. Then take a deep breath, and while exhaling, recognize a feeling of confidence and security rising within you, as you return to full consciousness, and slowly open your eyes.

Record any interesting information in your journal now. Again, as before, try to write down as many details as you can, as well as your emotional responses.

Expanding Your Horizons

You have just made tremendous strides in opening to your spiritual greatness! Releasing fear and accepting your intuitive power is a major step in your growth. Fear stands in the way of all of our dreams. It can stop us from trusting our spiritual guidance when it comes to us. When you feel yourself fearful in any way or for any reason, repeat this reflection. You will find it most useful in eliminating any and all fears and opening up that intuitive channel deep within you!

When you have embraced your growth, taking full responsibility for your joy, you are truly living an enchanted life! Your horizons expand, and you become more than you were. When you open to the realm of all possibilities, you open to the limitless gifts of the Universe. Even though responding to situations from your intuitive and psychic mind seems foreign at first, the more you practice, the faster you will get past your skepticism. Magic can't happen in an atmosphere of doubt and disbelief. Create an atmosphere of wonder and an openness to the fact that anything can happen in a Universe of all possibilities. Get rid of what's stopping you by moving past your fears, and—like magic—the good times will roll!

Affirmation 5

Affirm the following with enthusiasm, and repeat until you *believe* it:

"I am ready and willing to release my fears and create a magical life. I listen to my intuition, the voice of Spirit within me, as I create a life of abundance, joy, peace, and love. And so it is!"

Step 6

Share the Wealth

Teach others what you have learned

The object of this step is to expand your consciousness by giving back to the world what you have received. If you will recall, the Universal Law of Return or Circulation tells us that what we give we receive, and that what you give comes back to you tenfold. This applies to sharing your material wealth when and where it is needed, but it is also important to keep goodness in circulation by sharing that goodness, as well. Sharing our knowledge about living a life connected to our spirit means not only living life magically, but helping others live it, too. That is why I have written this book. So many people I have come to know in the last ten years want to live differently, but haven't the slightest clue as to how to do that. When you find your path, the fastest way to move along is to give others the benefit of your experience. In this, the sixth step on our journey, we will explore this concept of sharing all that we have and all that we are with the world, by recognizing and understanding our individual life purpose.

It might not be necessary for you to hang out a shingle and found a metaphysical center, because not all of us are meant to follow that path, but we all are meant to serve each other. The way you do it will be right and perfect for you.

In its simplest form, sharing the wealth of your spirit with others can mean that you treat them as you would like to be treated. This is not always an easy thing to do, especially when some rude salesperson irritates you, but that will be your true test of faith. If you can still treat others with respect, even when it seems that they don't deserve it, you will find that magically, there will be fewer moments in your life when these events occur. Remember, the Universe gives you more of what you give out. There will always be difficulties and disagreeable people out there in the world, but view them as teachers, set your emotions aside, take a deep breath and a big gulp, and try to remain calm. You will be truly rewarded with peace and less stress using this method.

From the simple state of sharing our goodness with others, we can move on to taking an active part in making the world a better place. You can volunteer your services in any number of ways: serving the elderly, homeless, your church or temple, animal shelters, or environmental groups. I'm sure you have heard this all before, but maybe not in the context of fulfilling your spiritual goals.

Talking with people who need spiritual counsel is another way to serve your soul. Listen to people who need your help, and advise them as to how they may begin their own spiritual journey. Recommend this book or others like it to help get them on track. Most of all, be willing to assist and to explain, although there is a danger here. An overzealous seeker can overwhelm someone who is not prepared for metaphysical information.

I have often had to tone down my own delivery. It seems that at every party or event I go to, someone will ask me a very profound question. As soon as they discover my occupation, they have a million questions about God, spirituality, and magical living. They are intrigued with the possibility of having it all, but are usually incredulous. I have to fight the urge to over-explain about the whole spiritual lifestyle—that is the danger I was talking about. It is wonderful to have the opportunity to talk to others about your journey, but it is equally important to not force them to accompany you. I can't tell you the number of times I have been confronted by religious zealots who have decided that my eternal soul is damned and that it is their job to save me. Their idea of salvation tends to be yelling and quoting the Bible. An extreme image, I know, but worth considering when making your own presentation.

Spreading the word of your spiritual joy requires restraint and consideration. Essentially, what you share when you talk about your beliefs is love. That is how all messages of faith should be delivered—with love. Do that and you can't go wrong.

The Magic of Your Life: Your Life Purpose

There is a reason why you were born. Okay. Now you can stop wondering about that. That should be a relief. You didn't show up here on the planet just to take up space and use natural resources. You came with a plan and a purpose—a life purpose. That is the metaphysical term for the reason you're alive. Very heady stuff, but it is time you began thinking about how you are going to share this magical experience with others. I have already said that our overarching purpose for living is to honor our Creator and to serve others, and in doing so we serve our soul. How does one know what one's life purpose is? This takes some time to figure out, because it not as obvious as it may seem.

Most people assume that their life purpose is directly related to their career. Wrong. It is true that many of us, myself included, have careers in the spiritual arena, but that still does not mean that we are fulfilling our life purpose in the course of our jobs. The reason for our being is far more expansive and much less limiting than any occupation. I'll explain.

For instance, a person's life purpose may use his/her career as a tool. I read recently about a man who owns a car wash. Now you're thinking, "What's so spiritual about a car wash, and how is that a life purpose?" Every occupation is a spiritual expression, and every job, career, business, trade, or calling is sacred because everything has been created by God. That should be a simple concept to grasp, so if that is true, than even a car wash is blessed—especially the one I am talking about. At this car wash, the owner admitted that he made a tidy living, and wanted to give back to his community. On Saturdays, this man washes the cars of single moms in his town, for free. It seems that he was raised by a single, hardworking mom, who struggled to raise him and his siblings. It is his way of honoring his mother and all mothers. This is a totally selfless loving act, motivated by his spirit. This is his life purpose. He was put here to honor and help those less fortunate—in particular, mothers in need. His life purpose is not to run a car wash. Do you see the difference? The car wash is blessed because it enables him to fulfill his life purpose by affording him a handsome income, so that he can easily afford to do his spiritual work.

Our life purpose is our greatest way to share the wealth of our spirit. There is a small snafu when it comes to knowing what our life purpose is. We must discover it. That is part of our spiritual journey. Understanding it and then acting on it is a great part of our path. It is not enough to simply learn about our spiritual nature. It is much more important to live it. That is the magic that changes a meaningless existence into a joyful, magical experience.

What's a Body to Do?

I use the above title purposely. Your body must do the physical work of your spirit. That is why it must be in good shape, healthy, and balanced. We have work to do on Earth, and we must have the necessary equipment in working order to do so. But beyond physical health, we must know that living our magical life requires a commitment to finding out what our spiritual life purpose is and than making it a reality in this world. How do you find out what your life purpose is? You focus your attention on it. Anything we focus our attention on becomes real in our lives. So how do we go about it?

Discovering your life purpose is a much easier task than you might expect it to be, but you must decide that you will be totally honest with yourself in the process. You will have to ask yourself some deep, penetrating questions, and you must be ready for the answers, no matter how painful they might be. I am not trying to frighten you, but if you are ready for this kind of soul searching, you are ready to handle the consequences. That is the mark of the spiritual warrior!

I have a method that I have used with myself and my own students which has proven successful in discovering life purpose. The three basic steps are listed as follows:

- Do a life assessment.

- Pray and affirm your desire.

- Meditate and focus your intention.

The Life Assessment

First, do a life assessment. That is the logical part of the process. With paper and pencil in hand, sit down in a quiet place. Allot at least fifteen minutes for this activity. Write down the following questions in your spiritual journal, and answer them honestly.

- What are the activities I love to do? (Don't censor anything, just list them.)

- How can I serve others while doing them?

- Do I have any talents or skills that I would like to share with others?

- Is there a special charitable gift I would like to give to other people? (Think of our car wash hero for this one.)

- Do I have a soft place in my heart for a particular group of people in need, or animals, or the Earth? What can I do to help?

Let's take a look at each one of these questions. What are the things you like to do, how can you serve others while doing them, and do you have any talents or skills that you would like to share? These questions all work together. A friend of mine likes to play softball in his off-work hours. It's a passion of his and he is very good at it. He gets so much enjoyment from playing that he wanted to share that feeling with others. To do that, he chose to coach a Little League team. Sharing his love brings him even more joy now, when he sees the delight and confidence in the kids. His "day job" is as a retail store manager, but his life purpose is to help children develop self-esteem, self-confidence, and pride in themselves. Now that's some purpose!

The last few questions can all be considered together, as well. Is there a special charitable gift you would like to give to other people like our car wash owner? Do you have a soft place in your heart for a particular group of people in need, or animals, or the Earth, and what can you do to help? Some peoples' life purpose is to protect and nurture animals. Three members of my church possess such a purpose. They have all been extremely active in the local SPCA, working tirelessly for needy, abused, and abandoned animals. Loving these creatures as they do, they feel compelled to help by some inner force that drives them to take care of these innocent beings. The way to tell that this is their purpose is that they have no choice but to help in this area, for if they did not, they would feel unfulfilled and guilty for withholding their care. All three of these people already take care of people in their chosen careers. Two are teachers and one is a therapeutic massage therapist—all jobs that focus on serving others. But their purpose in life seems to find its demonstration with the animals—something they do for free.

Not all life-purpose activities are done for free. You might be fulfilling yours while at work. For instance, the occupations that naturally serve, such as the clergy, nursing, medicine, or teaching, can reflect the life purpose of those practicing them. Mother Teresa is a case in point. A nun, she was already in service to God and humanity, but her contribution within that field was tremendous. It is easy to see how she fulfilled her life purpose. In my own life I have worked at many occupations, as a TV weather anchor, teacher, actor, director, singer, corporate account executive, and director of a nonprofit center, to name a few. Even my jobs now as minister, pastor, intuitive holistic counselor, channel, medium, and psychic artist are not the true fulfillment of what I feel is my own life purpose. You are reading it, and if you have been present at one of my lectures, you have heard it. I feel that my reason for being alive is to share my knowledge of spiritual and metaphysical concepts with others, so that they may find their own way to God. And I feel I do this best as a writer and inspirational speaker. My other talents and skills, and the jobs I've had in the past, have led me to this moment. All that I have done and learned now serves me as I live my true purpose, much as that car wash enables our giving proprietor to do his work. All you have accomplished and lived through, whether a job or a life experience, trauma, or the accumulation of lessons learned for having lived as long as you have, are all meant to serve you when you actually set out to actively live your life purpose. That brings me to synchronicity.

Synchronicity is a term that the great psychologist, Carl Jung, coined. What we believe to be coincidence is not that at all. According to Jung, all the events of our lives have been engineered by our Spirit to unfold in certain ways, and at certain times, keeping in flow with our purpose. There are no coincidences, and as you might have heard many times before, everything happens for a reason. The reason for the happenings is to enable us to learn our lessons and to fulfill our life purpose.

Synchronicity happens in your life when events and circumstances seem to inexplicably unfold in just the right and perfect order, just in time for you to benefit from them. We notice the synchronistic events in our lives because they seem like coincidences, but the difference is that they have a deeper, more profound energy around them. When they occur the usual response is one of awe and wonder.

Prayer and Affirmation

This is a simple step, and one with which you are very familiar. If you need to discover your life purpose, and are not clear in discerning it through your hobbies or skills, the best way to find it is through prayer. Metaphysicians use affirmative prayer, as I have used in the affirmations included in each chapter of this book. The affirmation at the end of this chapter will serve to help you to clear your mind of clutter and focus it on finding your life purpose. Putting this thought out into the Universe every day until you know what it is you came here to do will draw the realization of it faster than anything else I know!

You can also augment your affirmative prayer with any other prayers that feel right to you, from any religion or spiritual philosophy. Use whatever resonates with you and makes you feel as if you're getting your message out to God. If you need help understanding or writing affirmations, get a copy of my book, *How To Get Everything You Ever Wanted*. It explains the construction of affirmations from A to Z, and chapter 13 lists over a hundred of them, should you get too frustrated trying to write your own.

Meditation

The final method of understanding your life purpose is meditation. Meditation focuses your mind upon your intention. In this case, your intention is to discover and live your life purpose. When you get quiet, you allow your higher consciousness to speak to you. It speaks through subtle realizations and gentle outward signs in your environment that let you know which road to take to achieve the true fulfillment of your soul. Use the reflection in this chapter as your life-purpose meditation, and then look for the results to present themselves to you in your daily life. A book might come to you, or good advice from a friend may do the trick and trigger your understanding. The meditation will send a signal to the Universe that you are ready to know why you are here, and to take action on it. The rest will be revealed to you.

Share and Share Alike

The ultimate, holy purpose for your being born on to this planet is to share and distribute the wealth of your life where and when it is needed. Your practical life purpose enables you to do that. You have been working on it since your birth. Some people complete their purpose early in life and leave the planet young. Others don't even begin to serve in their full capacity until their death. We can see this demonstrated in the death of babies or stillborn infants. This is a tragedy, of course, but the soul that was the child fulfilled its life purpose by sharing its short life and then through dying. This concept meets with shock from my students, which might be yours when you read this, but nonetheless, I believe it to be true. The child-soul's purpose might just have been to facilitate a lesson for its parents, or to help on a global level, to serve all children. For example, if a child is stillborn, the parents were served by its presence in the womb and later, by rebuilding their lives after the death. This might have been a lesson that these parents wished to learn, and the child-soul agreed to be an instrument of their learning. These parents might go on to establish a support group for others in the same grief situation, or help the medical community get to the heart of the problem. The sharing goes on and on. No life is wasted, and none is without purpose.

Just a reminder: Remember, your life purpose is just a tool given to you by Spirit to assist you in serving God, the world, and all of God's creations. It is not your career, your dream, or your vocation. It is, rather, your soul's drive to love and serve expressed in human form and experience. It is your sacred mission.

When I think of fulfilling life purpose late in life, at the point of death, I think of the actor, Rock Hudson, who died of AIDS. We know that he had a long and noteworthy career, and while he is remembered for his great talent, he is known more for his death. He was the first celebrity in this country to disclose the conditions of his health, at great personal and professional risk, in order to prevent others from contracting this terrible disease. His disclosure opened the door to AIDS research in this country, gave countless victims of the disease a means of medical treatment, and above all, restored hope and respect. As an actor he made a great contribution to the film industry and to all his fans, but as a dying champion he truly fulfilled his purpose.

Your life purpose may not be as dramatic as Rock Hudson's, or even that of Christopher Reeve, who is using his celebrity status to find a cure for spinal injuries, his true-life purpose, yet it is equally important. Yours might seem small in comparison, but I assure you it is not. Raising children who have a major contribution to make to the world might be yours, or it might be to help one or two individual souls, but whatever it is, it is holy and blessed, and it is your sacred obligation to God and the world to fulfill.

Reflection 6
Unveiling Your Life Purpose

As I have said earlier, your life purpose has been part of your soul since before your birth on to the Earth. It is a matter of unveiling what is already there in your subconscious, so that you can begin to live it and experience your magical existence. This reflection and meditation will help you discover your life purpose. Be open and ready to receive the clues the Universe will give you, and make a commitment to act on your intuitive prompting, and what your heart is revealing to you.

As with the other reflections, assume a comfortable sitting position.

Now, once again, close your eyes, take three
gentle breaths, and relax, allowing the relaxation
to move from the top of your head all the way
down to the tips of your toes. Reflect upon the
following:

> As you breathe gently, relax and allow all thoughts to
> slowly subside from your mind. As you focus on your
> breathing, tell yourself that you are now open and ready
> to receive messages from the Universe concerning your
> life purpose. Ask your higher consciousness for guidance
> to lead you to the perfect circumstances, so that you may
> understand your purpose. Reflect upon your talents and
> skills for a moment. Upon which does your mind seem to
> focus? Register that thought, and move on. Now, gently
> allow your mind to think of the situations in the world
> that most inspire compassion within you. Register that
> thought, and move on. Spend a moment now thinking
> about what you most love to do in life, whether it is a job,
> hobby, or relaxation activity. Register that thought also.
> Now, simply breathe and relax in silence for a few
> moments, letting go of all thoughts. Know that the Uni-
> verse has heard your request for guidance and is answer-
> ing it as you enjoy this moment of peace. When you are
> ready, tell yourself that you will look for the signs of your
> request materializing in your world, and thank God for
> enabling you to find your way. Then take a deep breath,
> and, while exhaling, return to full consciousness, and
> slowly open your eyes.

Record any interesting information in your
journal now. Again, as before, try to write down as
many details as you can, as well as your emotional
responses.

Just a Matter of Time

It is just a matter of time now until you recognize what you love to do, what fulfills you as a person, where your heart is, and what you must do to accomplish your very personal sacred mission. Take a long, objective look at your life, all that you have done and learned, and see it as a means to an end. Each moment has been directed by your soul. I know that all that I have done in the past has led me to this moment in time. Even the painful experiences have been spiritually engineered by your higher consciousness to help you learn your lessons and acquire knowledge that you will need to fulfill your divine purpose in this lifetime. Try to see how all of your life experiences have led you to this moment. When you can see the patterns of your life experiences, follow their prompting by accepting your past and opening to your future. You will then be given both material and intuitive signs as to how to proceed. Listen and follow them to your destiny.

Affirm the following with enthusiasm, and repeat until you *believe* it:

Affirmation 6

"From this moment, I commit to my
sacred mission in life, and vow to
share all aspects of my life—material, physical, emotional, and spiritual—with the world and its inhabitants. My divine life purpose becomes
clear to me now, and I joyfully fulfill
it. For this, I give thanks to God. And
so it is!"

Step 7

Express Your Spirit

Live sincerely, honestly, and with integrity

Theater legend has it that George Abbott, a famous and well-respected director, was confronted by one of his actors during rehearsals for a Broadway show. The actor was having a tough time coming to grips with why he should enter from a particular doorway. As some temperamental actors do, he was not satisfied with just following the direction as it was given. Instead, he was determined to know why he was required to enter from that specific door, so he interrupted the rehearsal, faced Mr. Abbott head-on, and asked, "What's my motivation?" In his calm and determined way, the director answered, "Your paycheck!"

Now, I ask you, "What's your motivation? Why do you want to pursue a magical life?" It seems like a strange question, doesn't it? Not really. Your answer might not be as obvious as George Abbott's, but I guarantee you, it will be as practical and dramatic, if you are really and truly committed to your spiritual growth. What I am talking about here is a matter of sincerity. In Step 7, I am challenging you to actually live this spiritual life to which

129

your soul has guided you. Here you will have to face the music and put all you have learned so far into practice in your life. In this phase, you will learn to be honest with yourself, examine your sincerity and willingness to overcome the temptations of your ego, and live these concepts you have studied and synthesized into your personal spiritual philosophy on a day-by-day basis.

Do you honestly want to live your life differently? Are you ready to make the necessary changes? Are you willing to do all that is necessary to live magically, or do you just think the whole thing is "cool?"

I need to take a moment here to talk about a pet peeve of mine. If you answered this last cool question with a "yes" I hope it was because the whole spiritual process is so attractive to you and that the prospect of living your life magically, sincerely, and honestly is exciting and spiritually fulfilling. I'm okay with that, but if you simply think that following this path will make you popular with your friends, or make you feel like one of the in-crowd, rather than a nerd, then I have a problem.

In over a decade in doing this work, I have run into a lot of what I call "pseudo-spiritualists." These are people who insist that they have psychic abilities beyond compare, endeavor to tell me and everyone else around them how very spiritual they are, sputter the New Age lingo all over the place, tell you how sad the local mall is because the energy there is so negative, or insist that others don't understand them and their "gifts." It has been my experience that these folks are probably the least spiritual beings on the planet. They spend so much time thinking about how great and hip they are, but they have no time for God/Spirit. They think they are amazing and forget that their gifts come from an amazing Source. They have many lessons to learn. Do everything you can to recognize them before you follow their lead. Truly spiritual people don't talk much about it. They live it.

I'm asking you to be honest with yourself. This is no easy undertaking because when you finally dedicate your life to the spiritual path you take on a very challenging role. You must be ready and able to reexamine your motives for doing everything! Sounds like a pain in the neck. Well, sometimes it is. It's so much easier to go on living in a world of delusion and denial than it is to continually remind yourself that you are here to learn and grow, as difficult as that is at times.

Your motivation to pursue a spiritual life has to make sense to you, resonate with you and your beliefs, and feel right. When I ask my students why they are pursuing their path, they have trouble answering. One of them, who shall remain nameless, responded that he wanted to "help others." I told him that was nice, but weak. Then I asked him again what his real reason was. Reluctantly, yet thoughtfully, he said that he wanted to expand his consciousness so that he could overcome his fears of continuing to live as an alcoholic, fears of poverty, and loneliness. A far cry from helping others, don't you think? I explained to him that once he came to grips with his true motivation to release his own demons, he would be better equipped to help others and that would be a natural outcome for an enlightened soul.

As this student did, you must be willing to examine closely and face your true motivations for seeking the spiritual path or you will continue to live in a fantasy world, wondering why you can't seem to help anybody, not even yourself, even though you have the best of intentions. The best of intentions will do you no good if you do not clearly face the reasons why you want to make the changes and find your magic.

There is a culprit within all of us that can keep us from seeing our true motivations. Its name is Ego. If you are motivated by your soul to move forward for all the positive reasons, you will have to be willing to do one very important and essential thing—abandon your ego. In other words, get over yourself.

Let Go, Ego!

"Excuse me!" you say? Yes, that's right. You'll have to excuse yourself, or rather your ego, from playing a major part in making life decisions, responding to relationship problems, dealing with friends and relatives, coping with your finances, etc. Your ego is not necessarily negative in and of itself, it is just when it gets out of control that it presents a problem to your soul's development.

One of the functions of our ego is to assist us in choosing a value system. Yes, we choose our values. We decide what is right or wrong for us based on the stimuli in our environment. So, when we are in the process of creating our reality we rely on our ego to help us make those choices. For instance, a child grows up in a particular area of town. Maybe it's not such a great area. Let's say it's a slum. Well, this child has value choices to make. He or she might choose to accept the slum as his or her reality because it's convenient, he or she has learned to cope with it, and it takes no effort to continue to live in this fashion. The ego has accepted defeat. A stronger ego at work inspires one to get out of the negative situation and make a better life, no matter how difficult it might be. That ego has accepted growth.

The ego can work either way. Getting past the negative workings of the ego requires you to live a life that is other-centered, rather than self-centered. That is not to say that you never consider your own needs first, or sacrifice yours for the needs of others. Being other-centered means that you respect the needs and wants of others as *equal* to your own. Then everyone becomes your brother and you do not feel the temptations of the negative ego to be excessively competitive, without compassion, or dishonest. Rather, a healthy ego welcomes the successes of others, is encouraging, compassionate, and truthful. Can you see how this will lead to expansion of the Spirit? It should be quite clear.

The dark side of your ego can keep you locked in a limited consciousness, unable to discover your life purpose, or to make your contribution to the world, because you're too wrapped up in you to help anyone else. Here is that sincerity thing again. Are your motives for pursuing your spiritual journey sincere, and are you eager to discover and enrich your own life experience on this planet, as well as that of all other living things? If so, yours is an ego in check and the mark of a true seeker.

The ego is not necessarily bad or destructive. You need it to give you a sense of self-worth and self-esteem. Our ego, when it's working in our highest good, encourages us to feel happy and satisfied with ourselves and our accomplishments in life. These are not bad things. The negativity sets in when all we can think about is how we can benefit, or what we will get out of any situation. We become too attached to results and block our flow when our ego is out of control. It can blind us to the good around us and keep us trapped in our mind. It can also keep us from acting with integrity, because we are consumed with our own well-being, and not the least bit interested in anyone else's!

Join Your Own Club

The great Groucho Marx was said to have made the statement, "I'd never belong to a club that would have me as a member!" Ouch, Groucho. Unfortunately, many of us feel that way. We don't value ourselves enough to believe that we deserve the best in life. So, I say to you, join your own club! Get on your own bandwagon! March in your own parade! Okay, I'm getting a little crazy here, but it is crucial to understand that living a magical life requires you to like you! When you can look at your life and tell yourself you did the best you could and from this moment on you'll do better, you are liking yourself. That's it. That's all. No big deal. Just accept you the way you are, and resolve to do better. This is a major step for many of us, but it must be done if you intend to improve your life. Better still is that when you accept you, you begin to live with integrity, with uprightness, sound judgment, incorruptibility, adhering to moral values and personal truth. Think about it. When you don't value yourself you don't have any energy to pursue your dreams and create the life you want because you're too depressed to do anything. Sincerity and integrity go right out the window!

To know if you're ready to follow a spiritual path you must ask yourself these questions, "Am I a person others can trust and respect?" "Do I always try to act in the highest good of *all* concerned?" "Do I walk-the-walk, and talk-the-talk?" Here's the killer question, "*Am I a person I can love, trust, and respect?"* Would you join a club that would have you as a member?

The Best Example

You. You are the best example of God/Spirit in motion. You are the one walking on the Earth, the one going to work, the one caring for your loved ones, raising children, teaching, preaching, coaching, learning, and doing all the simple but profound things we do every day. It is fitting then that you be the example of a spiritual life well lived. It is tough to be a role model, but somebody's got to do it. Why not you? When you live in harmony with your soul, you are a natural example of joy and love. You really don't have to do anything special to show that to others. You are it. It is you. Everyone will know who you are. You know these people whom you feel are just a joy to be with; you might even have one living in your household. They are the embodiment of their beliefs, and the product of their thoughts and actions. Sincerity and integrity are attractive. People flock to a loving heart. Remember that when you're thinking about doing something you might not be proud of. Think twice and act nice. Soon it will take no effort at all.

Day by Day . . .

As odd as it may sound, there are things you can do each day to expand your consciousness. The root of consciousness unfolds at its own pace within us—it can't be forced, but it can be encouraged, helped along. If you are used to being negative or self-centered all the time, you can reverse those behaviors. Anything that is learned can be unlearned or changed. This is good news. In my classes my students have often asked for the nuts-and-bolts of what to do each day to stay on the path. I only tell them what I do and what works for me. It is with their encouragement that I offer these simple behaviors to you now. Give them a try and you will see your life changing for the better around you, just like magic!

For starters, here are some general behaviors that have helped make my life magical.

Develop Your Intuitive Abilities

Start today to use your inner knowledge, your gut feelings, to make decisions. Get out of your head and into your heart. You have heard me say this many times, but actually doing it is a lot tougher. Take baby steps and start now.

Open to New Vibrations Around You Without Fear

Just because you might encounter someone who doesn't see life the way you do, does not mean their negativity will rub off. Be brave! You just may influence them in a more positive direction by not judging them or their attitudes. Try to be open-minded, even if you don't agree with someone. There is always something you could learn about yourself in the process. People come into our lives for a reason. Try to see what that reason is, and use it to grow your soul.

Accept Change

When you set out on the path of spiritual discovery, change is inevitable. So many people have such a difficult time with it, but change is not always negative. I see change as a good experience and look forward to what exciting learning is ahead of me. If you see it as positive it will be so.

Become a Modern-Day Mystic

Living a spiritual/magical lifestyle is not any harder than living normally, but it requires a more focused effort and awareness. Whatever the effort, it is worth it because the payoff is huge! How about this for results: a life that is joyful, harmonious, loving, abundant, prosperous, and balanced. Achieving this reward means that you choose to live your life continually conscious of the implications of your thoughts, words, and actions. It is just like driving a car—when you get used to all the components and how they work, you won't even have to give it a second thought. Your spirit will express itself automatically, with very little effort from your conscious mind. For those of you who are still not quite sure how to get behind that wheel, so to speak, here are the tools to use:

- Put God first.

- Listen to your intuition.

- Meditate.

- Pray.

- Look for your lessons.

- Keep your mind and heart positive, loving, and open.

- Stay committed.

- Hang out with people who support and embrace your beliefs and values.

This list gives you the overall picture of how you should be conducting yourself each day. Yet, there is more. There's always more, and that's a good thing! My students were relentless, though, and insisted that I tell them exactly what I do each day to express my Spirit. In addition to the above, I do the following:

- Each morning when I rise, I head for my sacred space and make my connection with God. This contact consists of my sitting before my altar for about fifteen minutes. On less busy days I can stretch this into a half hour. During this time, I literally talk to God, out loud. Here is what I say: "I thank Spirit for all that I have, and all that is yet to come into my life."

- Then I tell God how I felt about the day just past and about the one ahead. I chat as though my best friend were with me, and by the way, She or He is. (This is great therapy for the soul. Although you may not get an immediate answer as you would from an earthly therapist, it is very cathartic to let God know just how you feel. Try it. It works wonders if you truly believe you are being heard, but even if you don't believe, you *are* being heard.)

- After that, I begin my prayer time. I pray for my needs, those others on my prayer list, and my family and circle of friends.

- Then I open to receiving the greatest good of the Universe. I literally set myself up for a good day by affirming: "I am open to the best the Universe has to offer me today. I receive it, and I accept it, and so it is!" Then I add, "This is going to be a positive and loving day, no matter what happens. And so it is!"

- I end my prayer by asking for guidance from God to handle the day well, and thank God for help in fulfilling Divine Will that day. "Use me, today, God. Show me how to express You and do our work today. For this, I give thanks. And so it is!"

- When all my prayers are done, I go into a short meditation, anywhere from five to thirty minutes, depending upon the time constraints of the day. Five minutes is plenty. If you have the luxury of more time, even better, but you can get a very peaceful benefit from calming yourself every morning, even if it's just for a few moments. You'll see the huge difference it makes in the way you approach your day.

When my persistent students tried these tips they were happy to report success. One of them said that her whole attitude toward life has changed because she now starts her day in a spiritual way. She feels she's not alone and that God is with her. Her connection or sense of God is more real to her now. It will happen for you, too.

As if that were not enough, my enthusiastic students wanted more. "That's great for starting the day," one woman said, "But what do you do to live magically and spiritually during the rest of the day?" A good question, for which I do have an answer. I proceeded to respond with my own way of dealing with the day in a spiritual way. It's my daily upkeep that enables me to stay focused and God-centered. Here's what I do *during* the day:

When presented with the opportunity to exercise and express my spirituality, I take it.

For example, do you know what a pain it is when you're trying to pull out of a crowded parking lot, like after a baseball game or something? Well you can express your Spirit in a very simple way. Let someone else go in front of you. You can do that at the market, or anywhere else, for that matter. This seems like a small action, but it packs a spiritual wallop, because you took advantage of the opportunity to do something good. Another thing you can do is give someone a compliment. It won't diminish you, and it could make their day. There are hundreds of things you can do. Watch for these simple but powerful moments throughout your day.

I use my intuition to make all my decisions during the day.

Whether it's a choice to get a pizza or Chinese for lunch, or what to spend on groceries, I exercise my intuitive muscle. I allow my inner wisdom to relay a message to me even while making simple choices. This takes practice because you need to be still and perceive the silent prompting. Usually, I ask myself an uncomplicated, "yes-or-no" question like, "Do I want pizza for lunch?" Then I literally wait to see if any doubt creeps up. If I begin trying to rationalize it by justifying my choice, then I know I don't want it in the first place. This justification takes the form of logic. You tell yourself you just had pizza yesterday, maybe you shouldn't have it two days in a row, you're getting fat and better cut down, etc. That's too much thought. Just hold the idea of pizza in your mind, be still, and see if you have any anxiety attached to it in the pit of your stomach. If not, go have a slice and forget the logic.

If on the other hand, your stomach starts to tingle, nerves start to activate, and you feel generally uneasy with the thought, go for Chinese. Do that with everything and you'll never eat a meal you don't want again! (Needless to say, use it for everything else, too!)

I face my day with the idea that I will move through it with all its challenges and rituals, responding from a place of wisdom within me, not fear.

Don't be afraid of what might happen. Be ready to deal with what does—no matter what.

I affirm my positive thoughts all day.

I say specific affirmations I might be working with, whenever I get a chance. Or, I just affirm my gratitude and joy in being alive.

I remind myself that I'm grateful for every moment I live on this Earth, and I try to see the wonder of Spirit in everything around me.

Every day, I bless everything—other people, my desk, my car, my home—everything.

A true test of my spiritual conviction every day is putting the needs of others on an equal par with my own. (I do this without compromising my own values. It keeps me balanced.)

If I am having a "bad" day, I try to do as much good as the bad to balance it. (This helps me sleep much better at night.) Most importantly, daily, I am constantly aware that my every thought, word, or deed affects everyone else, on some level, in some way.

I make every effort to perceive any problems that arise as solvable and temporary.

My emotions become my teachers during the day. They teach me about how I respond to life, and how to see things differently if I don't like my reactions.

I spend most of my day talking to God, and recognizing God as an active energy in every situation in my life, positive or negative, as though God was standing right next to me in physical form.

Sometimes I catch myself talking out loud in stores, thanking God for this or that. People look at me funny, but I feel good.

When my thoughts during the day don't serve my highest good, I change them into a positive perspective.

Each and every day, I actively invoke God's help, love, guidance, and grace into my life. In every moment, I am aware of the opportunity to express God and my gratitude for the honor of living yet another day.

I endeavor to be a walking, breathing expression of God's Divine Self on Earth.

Well, enough, don't you think? Don't be disheartened by it all. It does become second nature. It's just when you see it in print that it seems daunting, but really, it's fun and most of all, extremely fulfilling and joy-producing.

Just a Thought . . .

My friend Wanda once asked me how I find time to do anything else during the day besides my spiritual work. It seemed to her that I spent so much time at the spiritual work that I didn't have enough time for working, eating, or sleeping! She was amazed that I accomplished anything else during my day, and I can see her point. If you view your spiritual life as separate from your everyday life, her perception is accurate. But here's the thing—my Spirit *is* my day. It is who I am, not what I do. I firmly believe that we *are* spiritual, we don't *do* it. This made absolute sense to my friend, and I hope to you as well.

Reflection 7
Just What It Takes

Earlier in this chapter, I told you that living life in a spiritual and magical way would require a commitment. The commitment you will need to make will be to yourself, and it will be a challenge for you to keep. You must accept that you will do all it takes to live this life, sacrifices and all, in order for your highest good to manifest and for you to live in the constant state of joy. This reflection and meditation will help you discover just how much you're willing to do, and will offer you an objective look at yourself and your convictions.

As with the other reflections, assume your comfortable sitting position.

Now, once again, close your eyes, take three gentle breaths, and relax, allowing the relaxation to move from the top of your head, all the way down to the tips of your toes. Reflect upon the following:

> As you breathe gently, relax and allow all thoughts to slowly subside from your mind. As you focus on your breathing, tell yourself that you are now open and ready to receive messages from the Universe concerning your commitment to living a spiritual and magical life. For a moment, allow your mind to reflect upon the following characteristics of your personality. Think about how patient you are. Are you willing to take time to discover and uncover your spiritual potential? Are you too impatient to wait for results of your efforts? Does your ego often get in the way of your objectivity? Be honest with yourself and register your answers to these questions in your mind. Now, let's move on.

Gently allow your mind to think of the situations in your life that required your commitment. Were you able to stay focused? Were your motives sincere? How did it feel, being committed? Were you uneasy or comfortable with giving your word and holding to it, no matter what? Think about giving your word to yourself. Are you willing to promise yourself that you will give yourself the gift of a fulfilled, loving, abundant, prosperous, and joyful life, no matter what it takes to do it? Are you willing to promise the same to the God within you? Register those thoughts and your responses to them. Then take a deep breath, and while exhaling, return to full consciousness, and slowly open your eyes.

Record any interesting information in your journal now. Again, as before, try to write down as many details as you can, as well as your emotional responses.

Willing and Ready?

Congratulations. You have just faced the inner truth about your willingness to live a magical life in Spirit. If the answers you received for yourself in the above reflection were not to your liking, remember all you need do is change your perspective. Rethink your own belief system, and release your fears. Nothing can hurt you. You are the only one who can slow your progress. You must get out of the way of your soul's development. It's easy. You just have to want to. You have to have a strong desire to express Spirit sincerely, honestly, and with integrity each moment of your life. That's it. The following affirmation will help you become committed to this new life and stay that way. Say it every day, especially in your weakest moments when you feel your conviction sinking. When you utter these words, know that you have thrust yourself into the most exciting and fulfilling path your have ever undertaken. God bless you for giving the gift of a sacred life to yourself and the world!

Affirmation 7

Affirm the following with enthusiasm, and repeat until you *believe* it:

"I thank you, God, for the opportunity to be a living expression of You on this Earth. I release all blocks or fears I might have to living this new and magical existence, and I look forward to living in joy, peace, and grace for the rest of my life. And so it is!"

Step 8

Keep Learning

Continue to seek out and acquire knowledge

The human brain is capable of absorbing a tremendous amount of information. It is foolhardy to believe that once we find an ideology or spiritual philosophy to embrace, we can put the brakes on learning. In Step 8, I encourage you to continue your spiritual quest to learn and grow, to continue to seek out information and teachers, and to make your life a constant channel for wisdom. More than that, I'm giving you very definite meditation techniques to help you keep this wisdom channel ready to receive any and all transmissions. I'll walk you through my favorite meditations so that you can remain a magnet for attracting people and experiences that will grow your consciousness for the rest of your life, or for as long as you are a willing participant. Some of the greatest knowledge will come to you when you still your mind and allow God to speak directly with you. In this step, you are offered the opportunity to choose your deepest communication tool. It might just be one of the most important choices you make as you pursue your spiritual path.

147

I get very disheartened when I hear people say that they have learned enough—one can never learn enough. The whole idea of living spiritually implies continuous growth. If a person is of a mind that there is nothing left to learn, he or she puts a stop to the expansion of the Spirit. I am blessed with a small group of what I call "lifetime" students. These are folks that have been with me since I founded my church and center. I admire them because they are eager to continue learning and growing, and they make that a priority in their lives. We are all busy people, but in order to live magically we need to constantly increase our knowledge base and learn new ways to improve our lives to better enable us to recreate our reality.

It has been my experience that it is often necessary to change the way we do things. Progress, particularly spiritual progress, is vital to our happiness and the quality of our lives. Think of the energy you engender when you think constructive thoughts. Your mind creates your world. Doesn't it make sense to keep feeding it with new information?

Your Spirit is emerging. Seeking new ideas and knowledge enhances this process and enriches your soul. Some people feel as though they are not intelligent enough to absorb profound spiritual information. In fact, I know a lot of people who have big trouble with the Bible, let alone any other esoteric or religious text. Even though you may have trouble understanding some concepts, you should do what you can on your own, and make every attempt to affiliate yourself with others of like-mind who work with a good, loving, and generous teacher. Don't think that you are not smart enough to grasp these lofty concepts. When you study with the right teacher, you will. Ask God to guide you to a teacher or group that can help you. Before you know it, you'll be involved and learning. It can do wonders for the ego, as well as the brain.

Your Magical Mind

One of my secret wishes is to be able to teach spiritual-metaphysical concepts to everyone who wants to learn about them. That's one of the reasons I'm writing books. Your mind is a magical tool that can lead you to incredible heights of joy and fulfillment, if you will allow it to explore the realm of unlimited consciousness. There's a lot of information out there in the Universe, just waiting for you to tap into it. I wish I could step right out of this book and help each one of you, but that would be a bit time consuming. So, if I never have the pleasure of your Spirit in my classes and seminars, I am still determined to familiarize you with what I have found are some of the areas of study spiritual seekers should pursue.

The subjects I am including here have been most helpful and effective for my students in my own practice for the past decade or so. Here I've included spiritual methods of meditation that are extremely helpful and necessary for the seeker to master to move forward on the path. Later in the chapter, I've touched on the subject of intuitive-psychic development that will enhance your magical experience. It is my suggestion that you begin studying these areas. Address whatever feels right to you. Remember, use your intuition in deciding what information you wish to explore, and then take your time. Don't jump from one subject to another or try to study too many concepts at once. You'll only confuse yourself and scatter your energy, and you know what that can do. Now, take a gentle breath, relax, and let your higher self respond to the following forms of meditation.

Relax and Open

Meditation is a form of relaxation. It is rather uncompli-cated and very easy to do. Best of all, you can do it by yourself; no middleman needed here. You can do it any-where, any time. Meditation serves to calm and destress you, and enables you to access deeper levels of your mind and the unseen realm of Spirit. It is often labeled "going within," because meditation is silent and personal. Some people are afraid of it because they think they'll have a scary psychic vision or something mind-boggling will happen while they're in meditation. That does occur sometimes, but let me reassure you, there are no boogie men in your psyche waiting to jump out. You have to go to amusement parks for that, so don't be intimidated by your fears. Meditating is very easy. The most difficult part of it is putting a stop to nagging, intrusive thoughts that can distract you and throw off your focus. If you have been doing the reflection exercises in this book so far, you have been meditating. Reflection is one form of medita-tion, using a suggestion, question, or theme to focus your mind on one thought. When that is accomplished you are, in essence, silencing the clatter of your conscious mind and allowing your subconscious and higher minds to take over, just for the moment. This is the way spiritual folks open to the God within us.

There are an infinite number of meditation methods available to us, in addition to reflection. There is guided meditation, higher vibrational Om meditation, Eastern meditation (which can include Zen meditation, Buddhist meditation techniques, or Hindu, Shinto, and Yoga meditation), Transcendental Meditation (a throwback to the gurus of the sixties and seventies, but still very effective), Tantric meditation, Shamanic Journeying (the Native American form), stress-reducing meditation, spiritual energy healing meditation, meditation with music or without, and many, many others. Any one of these forms will be interesting, informative, and effective. You should explore the ones that attract you. Get to the library or the Internet and find the particular form. There are so many books on the subject that you'll be overwhelmed with choices. Stick to what resonates with your Spirit! I've listed several of my favorite meditation books in the bibliography. Give them a try, or find your own.

Choose or Lose

Meditation is part of my daily practice. I have my favorite techniques and now it's time for you to find yours. Don't miss out on this great spiritual tool. It is the mark of a true seeker to be skilled at silencing his or her conscious mind and accessing the deeply spiritual aspects of the self. Since you are now familiar with reflection mediation, for our purposes, I will focus on familiarizing you with the forms of basic meditation, guided meditation, spiritual healing meditation, chakra meditation, and Om meditation. What follows are descriptions of those forms that I give my private students who are not familiar with the process at all, in order to help them find their most comfortable and enjoyable process. If you are attracted to any or all of these meditations after reading the descriptions, you should explore them in depth by taking a formal class in meditation techniques, or joining a weekly meditation group. Calming your mind is a wonderful gift you should give to yourself regularly. You'll notice a difference in your physical, emotional, and spiritual well-being very quickly.

The Basics of Meditation

Breathing Meditation

The best way to begin meditating is to learn how to breathe deeply. This in itself is a form of relaxation that can greatly benefit your physical as well as spiritual well-being. When you begin meditating, you should sit upright in a comfortable chair, feet flat on the floor, palms either turned up or down, and resting on the lap. If you recline, you might fall asleep. That means you need more than meditation, you need rest! To keep alert it is best to sit up in your chair. The calming energy will flow from the top of your head all the way down to the tips of your toes. You should feel the relaxation as you breathe. There is no way that you will not notice the difference, especially if you're the nervous type. Make sure you are alone when you're meditating, at first, or in the learning stages, because others who do not understand your process might distract you. Turn off the phones, put the cat out, and relax. This is your moment to connect with the Divine within you. The following is the first form of meditation I use with my students:

> *Find a comfortable position in your chair, relax, close your eyes, and take three deep, cleansing breaths, inhaling through the nose and exhaling through the mouth. Do this at your own pace. As you breathe, relax your*

body, and allow all thoughts to gently fade from your consciousness, as you focus on breathing in . . .. and out . . . and in . . . and out . . . (When you focus on the breathing, there is no room in your mind for extraneous thought. Voila! You are meditating.)

This breathing meditation can be your most enjoyable one, especially if you are a person who has trouble calming your mind. If you are focusing on breathing in and out and paying attention to that, you cancel out other thoughts. This works well, I have found, for folks new to meditation. Do this meditation in this form for five minutes or so, for at least a week, at the same time of day in the same place in your home. This gives your psyche a sense of comfort and you get used to the process without the distraction of a new environment each session. Use this breathing meditation until you feel you are ready to move forward to bigger and better things!

It is important to allow yourself to become accustomed to meditating so that you can move on. The other forms of meditation will take you deeper into your mind, and enable you to access your higher consciousness. As you meditate often, you will find it easier and easier to drift into a deep trance state. You will derive the most benefits from your meditation in this advanced state of quiet and stillness. The ultimate aim is to make contact with the God within by relaxing enough to open to the flow of your inner wisdom from your higher mind to your conscious mind. This is the empowering purpose of meditation.

You can see that, in the early stages, meditation serves to relax you and help you to calm the body and mind. Through this relaxation technique you will eventually enable your mind to access the answers and solutions to your life's problems, and make conversing with God a common and everyday event in your life. That's magic!

Open-Eyed Meditation

The next best thing to a breathing meditation is the open-eyed meditation. I have taught this technique to busy executives who don't have much time to calm down during the day. This meditation can be done anywhere, and the beauty of it is that no one will even know you're doing it because your eyes are open! It can be done at your desk, at the lunch counter in the local diner, in the park, or anywhere in public, for that matter. You can even do it while waiting to get into the doctor's office. For your personal safety, don't try this while driving or operating heavy machinery. Do this meditation after you've pulled over to the side of the road. Then you can use it as a handy way to get a little relief on those long road trips. Of course, if you're a passenger, the point is moot. Here is the method:

> *Find a comfortable sitting position, and let your gaze fall upon a fixed object in the visual path directly ahead of you. Don't look to the side, or up or down, but rather find an object that is stationary, preferably small, like a doorknob, or crack in the wall, straight ahead in your vision. As you gaze at the object, take your three cleansing breaths and relax. Just gaze, don't stare, and relax your eye muscles in the process. Focus on the task at hand, keeping your gaze steady for a few moments. At the same time, keep breathing normally, and allow your thoughts to subside. If thoughts try to crowd in on you, simply remind yourself that you are meditating, close your eyes for a moment, open them, and realign your*

gaze again at the object. Keep this up for just a few
moments, until you recognize that you have noticeably
calmed down and are breathing normally. Then, when
you feel you are ready and relaxed, gently close your
eyes for a second, and when you open them, return to
the activities of your day.

You will be amazed at how relaxed you'll get doing this.
The executives I worked with couldn't get over how easy it
was to just sit for a moment and calm down. They tell me
they really need it after a hectic day's schedule or stressful
meeting. I'm sure it will do wonders for you, too.

Candle Meditation

Candles have been used for centuries during religious
rites, but they are really wonderful tools for meditation.
This meditation works much the same way as the above
technique, with eyes open, but now gazing at the flame of
a candle. The procedure is the same while the meditation
is in progress, but of course you can't do this just anywhere. My advice is to save the candle meditation for private moments at home. It can be so beautiful when done
at night or in a dark room. The hypnotic ambiance of the
candle's glow adds to the relaxation state, and many of
my students find that they like this feeling most. I enjoy it
myself, because the atmosphere at night is usually quieter
and more conducive to calming the mind.

In choosing a candle, pick a white one or one with a
color that soothes and calms, like purple or blue. The
point here is to create an atmosphere of serenity and
peace. Place the candle on a table or altar, if you have one
in your home. If not, dedicate a sacred space to keep your
candle, but be sure that you can sit right in front of it,

directly facing it at eye level, or slightly below. Craning your neck up or down will definitely kill the mood. Here's another little tip I happened to stumble upon after several candlesticks exploded before my eyes. Don't use glass! This fact dawned on me when a taper candle I had been using burned itself down into the holder while I was meditating. You can imagine my reaction. I thought God was trying to tell me something. It was, "Don't use glass!" Metal works best. There's nothing like being jolted out of your peace of mind by glass projectiles to teach you a valuable lesson. The really embarrassing part is that my eyes were wide open, as yours will be when you do this following meditation:

> *Find a comfortable sitting position, and let your gaze fall upon the candle directly in front of you. As you gaze at the candle flame, take three cleansing breaths and relax. Just gaze, don't stare, and relax your eye muscles in the process. Keep your gaze steady for a few moments. At the same time, keep breathing normally, and allow your thoughts to subside. If thoughts try to crowd in on you, simply remind yourself that you are meditating, close your eyes for a moment, open them, and realign your gaze again at the flame. Do this for just a few moments, until you recognize that you have noticeably calmed down and are breathing normally. Then, when you feel you are ready and relaxed, gently close your eyes for a second, and when you open them, thank the candle for its help, extinguish it, and return to the activities of your day.*

Guided Meditation

You might be familiar with guided meditation. This is the form in which a scenario is created for you. The scenario is then spoken live in meditation groups, or recorded on tape, to follow at will. The person delivering the meditation speaks slowly and deliberately, in a soothing voice designed to relax you. Then you are guided by the voice to release any stress in your mind, and to relax your body. Some of these mediations go from your head to your feet, relaxing each muscle group. These are great, especially if you have physical pain. You can purchase guided mediation tapes at your local bookstores.

Another source of guided mediation is a meditation group with a leader who facilitates the session. Many of these groups meet weekly or monthly, and it would be well worth your time and money to participate. Plus, you'll find people of like mind to hang out with. That's another great benefit. Kindred souls. You can find them by checking your local New Age bookstores or spiritual centers and churches, such as mine. In my Sunday meetings, guided meditation is done twice during the service, once for healing and then for opening to prayer.

You can also get a book of meditations, record them in your own voice, or have a friend who is theatrical do it for you. Then you can play them whenever you choose. I am not listing a guided meditation here because all the reflections in this book are simple guided meditations. They can be recorded for later use. Find those you feel are most significant for you as you read, record some of them, and use them whenever you want to work on that particular need, with my blessings.

Spiritual Healing Mediation

Meditation has long been used to heal the body. In ancient traditions as well as current practice, more and more holistic practitioners are witnessing the remarkable healing powers of the mind. My practice is no exception. I have worked with countless numbers of people who have healed their bodies using meditation and prayer. To me, the two are one. There are all kinds of spiritual healing meditations, depending upon one's particular spiritual bent or the individual teacher. We use the one that I like best every Sunday at our metaphysical worship services. It is a universal healing meditation designed to heal the body, mind, and spirit by opening an individual's spiritual channel to God, through relaxation. In the course of this meditation, you are asked to open to receiving the healing energy from Spirit into your body, heart, and mind, and are encouraged to help it along. Accepting the energy is the key here. Yet, remarkably, you don't have to accept or believe to be healed. That is the amazing reality. I have seen successful results with some of the most critical and negative people you could ever meet, yet they heal. This is the miracle.

If you are open and believing you create the ultimate climate in which spiritual healing can take place. You are essentially telling God that you are ready to give up the old life of pain and suffering because you don't need it anymore, and are ready for a new life of health and joy. You also imply that you are willing to accept your healing, and help others to heal as well. It is a truly generous gift we receive from God and one which Spirit wishes us to share. So, the mark of a spiritual seeker is the willingness to heal him- or herself, in all aspects, and to be an instrument of healing for others.

Here is my favorite spiritual healing meditation (a guided meditation). May you use it and be healed.

Relax, close your eyes, and feel a wave of relaxation moving from the top of your head, all the way down to the tip of your toes. Know that there is a circle of God's white light and protection all around you. Only loving energies many enter this circle, and no negativity is permitted here. As you relax, take a gentle breath, inhaling through the nose and exhaling through the mouth. Now, feel a ray of white light coming from the circle of white light all around you, entering in through the crown or your head. Feel it moving down your body slowly. Pull it to the area of your body that is in need of healing, at this moment. Feel the white light removing the pain and discomfort. Imagine it erasing the dis-ease as a laser would erase darkness. If you have an emotional problem, or your heart is heavy, allow the white light to surround your heart and comfort you. Surrender your pain to the light. If you are confused and it is difficult to make a decision, allow the light to surround your forehead, and feel it clearing your mind, and relieving the confusion. And, if you feel you are without Spirit, allow the white light to fill you with comfort, and know that you are one with God, and you are not alone. And as white light fills you, from toe to head, like water fills a glass, imagine it and feel it filling you up . . . up . . . up, until it reaches the top of your head. Now hold this light within you for a moment, and say to yourself, "I thank the Father-Mother God for this healing I have just received."

And now, in your mind's eye, envision the Earth as it is suspended in the darkness of the Universe. See the blue and white ball, as it gently rotates in the darkness of space. Feel a ray of white light moving out from your heart, out . . . out . . . out . . . into the Universe, moving up . . . up . . . up . . . through the ceiling of the building into space, and see it joining with the rays of white light from everyone who is praying around the world, at this moment, as it forms a halo of white light and healing around the Earth. The light is healing the Earth itself, the atmosphere, and all levels of life—animal, vegetable, mineral. Know that as you pray, the Earth itself is healed. And now, if there is anyone you know who is in need of healing, see this person in your mind's eye as whole and in perfect health. Know that as you pray, he or she is healed. Now say to yourself, "I thank the Father-Mother God for using me as an instrument of Your healing. I promise to take this message of healing light to everyone I meet, each day of my life. And so it is!" And now, take a gentle breath, inhaling the white light, and as you exhale return to full consciousness, and open your eyes.

Sometimes it's really hard to get the church membership back to consciousness after this one! It's very soothing and you may not want to come back, but please do. There's more to read.

Chakra Meditation

This is a more advanced method. If you're just starting out, I recommend sticking with the first four meditations, but you should know what tools are available to you as you continue on your journey. Without going into an in-depth explanation that could be the content of another book, briefly, this is what the chakras are.

In Sanskrit terms, they are defined as energy centers within the body. The Hindi believe that we have many of these within our body, but that there are seven primary centers. These seven energy centers are the source of our life force, or *prana*, and that by keeping these centers balanced, we can maintain good health, and live a harmonious existence. That is an oversimplification, but it is the basic idea.

The seven centers are aligned vertically along the body, projecting energy out into the Universe and forming what we sometimes call the aura, or auric field of energy around us. When any one of these centers is out of whack, we can experience disease, pain, discomfort, sadness, difficult situations, and the like in the corresponding areas of the body, mind, or life. It is said that, generally, the conditions that throw these areas out of alignment are self-induced or carried from other lifetimes. It is further believed that each chakra vibrates to a specific color of energy, and when this color is added to or subtracted from the afflicted center, it can balance itself.

For centuries, in order to balance the chakras and harmonize one's life with one's spirit, gurus have not started a day without their daily chakra cleansing and balancing routine. This form of meditation is good for those who have a background in spiritual studies and are moving along at a higher level of development. I usually cover this form with more advanced students, but here is a very basic chakra balancing meditation. Give it a try. You'll feel the results immediately.

> *Relax, close your eyes, and feel a wave of relaxation moving from the top of your head, all the way down to the tip of your toes. As you relax, take three gentle*

breaths, inhaling through the nose and exhaling through the mouth. As you breathe, imagine that you are surrounded by a circle of white light. Picture a ray of that white light moving in gently, into the crown of your head. As this white light enters the crown of your head, it turns a violet color. See it, a beautiful violet hue, as is settles at the crown of your head. Imagine that there is a beautiful violet rosebud there. Allow the bud's petals to slowly open a bit, and see and feel the rose gently rotating clockwise. Hold that image in your mind for a moment.

Now allow the violet light to move slowly down to your forehead. Feel all the muscles in your forehead relaxing as the light turns a beautiful indigo blue. Again, hold the indigo light around your forehead, and see a beautiful indigo rosebud at its center. Allow the bud's petals to slowly open a bit, and see and feel the rose gently rotating clockwise. Hold that image in your mind for a moment.

Now allow the indigo light to move slowly down your face to your throat. Feel all the muscles in your throat relaxing as the light turns a beautiful royal blue. Allow the blue light to surround your throat, as you relax all your throat muscles. See a beautiful royal blue rosebud at the center of the royal blue light. Allow the bud's petals to slowly open a bit, and see and feel the rose gently rotating clockwise. Hold that image in your mind for a moment.

Now allow the royal blue light to move slowly down your neck, over your shoulders, and down your arms, as you relax. When the light reaches your heart, it turns a beautiful vivid green. Feel all the muscles in your chest and upper back relaxing now. Allow the green light to surround your heart, as you release all worry, pain, and fear. See a beautiful green rosebud at the center of the green light. Allow the bud's petals to slowly open a bit, and see and feel the rose gently rotating clockwise. Hold that image in your mind for a moment.

Now allow the green light to move slowly down your chest to your midsection. Feel all the muscles in that area and around the lower back relaxing as the light turns a beautiful brilliant yellow. Allow the yellow light to surround your midsection as you relax your muscles. See a beautiful yellow rosebud at the center of the light. Allow the bud's petals to slowly open a bit, and see and feel the rose gently rotating clockwise. Hold that image in your mind for a moment.

Now allow the yellow light to move slowly down your body to your hips. Feel all the muscles in that area relaxing as the light turns a striking orange. Allow the orange light to surround your hips as you relax. See a beautiful orange rosebud at the center of the light. Allow the bud's petals to slowly open a bit, and see and feel the rose gently rotating clockwise. Hold that image in your mind for a moment.

Now allow the orange light to move slowly down your hips, down your body to your toes. Feel all the muscles in your throat relaxing as the light turns a vivid red. Allow the red light to flow down your body as you relax. See a beautiful red rosebud at the center of the light. Allow the bud's petals to slowly open a bit, and see and feel the rose gently rotating clockwise. Hold that image in your mind for a moment.

At this time, imagine and see in your mind's eye a picture of yourself as a rainbow of vivid, light. Relaxing in its glow, release all stress and pressure of the day. Hold that peace for a moment.

Now, gently and slowly return your focus to the top of your head. See the violet light once again. Allow it to slowly melt down and recede into the indigo light at your forehead. Next, imagine that the light is receding and moving down your face, and melting into the royal blue light at your throat. Feel the light gently receding down your throat, arms, and chest as it melts into the green light around your heart and upper chest. Relax as you imagine this green light moving down and melting into the vivid yellow light around your midsection. When the light reaches this area, it slowly recedes and blends into the orange light around your hips. After this, the orange light slowly recedes into the red light, which gently moves down your legs, to your ankles, over your feet, and out your toes and the soles of your feet, as the Earth absorbs any of the remaining light. You are now relaxed, refreshed, and at peace, as you take a gentle breath, and upon exhaling you return to full consciousness and open your eyes.

There you have a very basic chakra balancing meditation that will help you feel better and more in flow than ever!

Om Meditation

Spiritual masters have known that sound vibration can help us harmonize our body with our Spirit. *Om* is the Sanskrit word for God, and it is believed that when uttered, this most sacred word invokes that power within us, energizes us, and takes us to new levels of spiritual understanding and enlightenment. I know that when I use this form of meditation my whole body vibrates and I feel a tremendous surge of energy. My advanced students especially like this one, because they say that they go deeper into the meditative state using the Om than with any other form, and consequently have more satisfying and relaxing meditation experiences. I agree.

Even though the Om meditation sometimes manifests profound results in the moment, it is quite simple, so I have decided to include instructions here for you to try. You have to be ready to feel a little silly, because you will be humming to yourself—not something you might want to try with a house full of people. This is best done when you are alone, but I have experienced remarkable results when doing it in a group. The group energy multiplies and the whole room seems to be vibrating—very cool, but if the idea of this seems a bit too odd for you, or you are not ready for this level, just go back to the breathing, candle, and guided meditations. Don't rush your progress. Just allow it to unfold.

The following is the Om technique I use.

> *Find a comfortable sitting position, close your eyes, and take three cleansing breaths as you relax for a few moments. As you breathe normally, allow your thoughts to subside. If thoughts try to crowd in on you, simply remind yourself that you are meditating. Now gently take a breath, and as you exhale, sing a monotonal note using the word "Om." Sing the Om note for the full exhalation of your breath. Then inhale and repeat the sound, sitting peacefully and observing the vibrations*

going on in your throat, lips, face, and body. Do this for
at least eight or nine times (sacred numbers) as you
relax and observe. When you feel you are relaxed and at
peace, take a gentle breath, and as you exhale, return to
full consciousness and open your eyes.

The beauty of this meditation is that you will notice immediately that thoughts are not disturbing you because you are involved in the vibration. If you repeat it often, eventually you will not think at all, and you will find that the vibration carries you to higher planes of relaxation automatically. Then you will be able to release any spiritual blocks you might have and open to the gifts of the Universe. That is how we get past our logical reservations, and make ready for Spirit to enter our lives in full force. To work further with this type of meditation, do your research, find a group, or allow your Spirit to guide you.

Reflection 8
The Path to the Light

This chapter was loaded with specific meditations. I decided that we needed a reflection here to help us stay motivated to learn and grow, and to keep our consciousness active and moving forward, without reservation or blocks. You know that to grow in Spirit you must be willing to embrace learning and, most importantly, to be a teacher yourself when it is deemed necessary. To help us make ready for this grand and wonderful responsibility, I have included the following reflection and subsequent affirmation. Performing them will focus your mind on staying in the moment, and remaining receptive to insight from any source. They will guide you on your path and light your way to a future of joy, hope, promise, and love.

As with the other reflections, assume your comfortable sitting position.

Now, once again, close your eyes, take three gentle breaths and relax, allowing the relaxation to move from the top of your head all the way down to the tips of your toes. Reflect on the following:

> As you breathe gently, relax and allow all thoughts to slowly subside from your mind. As you focus on your breathing, tell yourself that you are now open and ready to receive wisdom from the Universe and to live in the light of Spirit. For a moment, allow your mind to reflect upon the level of your openness to new information, people, situations, and teachers coming into your life. Think about how ready you are. Are you willing to seek out new experiences to enhance your spiritual growth? Are you willing to give up old ways of thinking? Are you ready to engage in spiritual practices such as meditation to expand your consciousness? Be honest with yourself and register your answers to these questions in your mind. When you feel satisfied with your responses, take a deep breath, while exhaling return to full consciousness, and slowly open your eyes.

Record any interesting information in your journal now. Again, as before, try to write down as many details as you can, as well as your emotional responses.

Learn and Grow

Every effort that you make to seek out and learn new information along your spiritual journey will be rewarded with insight and growth. As you learn, your knowledge base grows, but so does your soul. The more enlightened your mind becomes, the closer you get to your spiritual goals. As you develop your meditation skills and intuitive abilities, your consciousness begins to accept new ways of thinking, and learns to use spiritual methods to solve life's problems. Staying open to all of the knowledge of the Universe will help you to continue to prosper and live a life that is unlimited in its capability and success. A life filled with wisdom and knowledge is a life lived to its fullest. It is truly magical.

Affirm the following with enthusiasm, and repeat until you *believe* it:

Affirmation 8

"I am open, ready, and willing to
learn and grow in wisdom and light,
expanding my consciousness, and being an instrument of learning when I
am needed. For this blessed gift and
fulfilling life, I give thanks to God.
And so it is!"

Did you ever know anyone who, when he or she walked into a room, others noticed immediately. These people exhibit a certain kind of charisma. They wear it around like a halo. Others will often say that these folks "glow" or "light up a room." You might even be one of these blessed individuals. If so, lucky you, for you are the walking, talking example of love on Earth. Did you ever think of that? People who shine and stand out in a crowd don't just have star quality; they exude from every pore an energy that is positive, hopeful, and loving. I'm talking about the men and women that you want to be around, the kind of person you wouldn't dream of excluding from your parties or gatherings. This special creature seems to attract loving people as friends, becomes successful at her or his chosen career, has enough money and possessions to live a balanced life, and is generally one whom most of us would envy. When this person is in the room, we feel it. We know he or she is there, because that quality of light and peace cannot be ignored. This is Spirit

Step 9

Exude Love

Be the embodiment of love on Earth

moving among us. Imagine how the people reacted to Jesus Christ as he moved through the little villages spreading his message of peace and love. He just couldn't be ignored. That's why he caused so much of a commotion. Loving people make waves. They cause a commotion. They're supposed to. Energy swirls around and through them like a gentle breeze that touches all who are privileged to cross their path. This is the end to which the spiritual speaker aspires. This is the emanation of Light (God).

In Step 9, I will give you the basic dynamics of living your life in a loving way, the actual steps to take and things to do to keep your life moving on the spiritual path, to help you live each day as the walking embodiment of love on Earth. This step will also help you to release any blocks to receiving and giving divine love so that you can live your life as a pure expression of Spirit, exuding love.

When I talk of exuding love, I'm really telling you that in order to do this you need to find that place within you that is at peace, and simply knows that there is an intelligence in the Universe that is guiding every moment, event, and circumstance of your life. This is easily said, but very hard to do. The good news is that once you get this concept your life will take on new and amazing dimensions. You'll find more joy in the mundane chores of life, and be less bothered when things don't seem to go your way. Staying on an even keel, in flow and balance, creates an aura of confidence that surrounds you. Your attitude changes because you are no longer looking for someone or God to blame for the circumstances of your life. A loving person accepts life as it comes, relies on God to get him or her through, and never, ever forgets that God is the source of all good in life. If everyone in the world got this message, what a wonderful world this would be! This is one of the primary messages one of my heroes, Beatle John Lennon, tried to express in his song "Imagine." Imagine if we could all give off love energy instead of fear, anger, or sadness.

One of my students asked one day how I managed to stay positive. I was very honest with her, and told her that I have my down moments, too, but thankfully they are few and far between. I told her that one day I just decided that I would be a living example of love on Earth.

I gave up being sad, lonely, angry, and afraid. Those energies were wearing me out and I couldn't accomplish what I wanted in life because my brain was too busy processing all that junk! When I cleared out the clutter, my world became magical. She liked the whole concept, but was still uncertain how to get to that point in her own life. I simply asked her this question, "How disgusted are you with yourself and your life?" You see sometimes, though not always, we need to be pretty disgusted to make a change. Now I ask you, "How disgusted are you?" Good and disgusted, I hope. Enough to change your world and work some magic?

Nuts and Bolts

I realize you're thinking, "Yes. Sounds good, but how do I do it, already?" Here's how:

Decide to put your energy into changing your life for the better.

This means that when you're good and disgusted, or just plain ready, you make a deal with the God within you to quit acting like a baby. You decide to take full responsibility for your life and all the junk that comes along with it. Today, this moment, resolve to be the person that you have always wanted to be. One of my favorite quotations, from Henry David Thoreau, reads, "What lies before us and what lies behind us are small matters compared to what lies within us. And when we bring what is within out into the world, miracles happen." Thoreau knew that to have a magical life, you need to think like a magician. Take leaps and risks and throw off old thinking. Unleash the power within you! That's the first thing you should do.

Be who you truly are, and let others see it.

Most of the time we're trying to be, as my mom likes to say, ". . . on our best behavior." This is not totally honest because it shields our true self from others. What we appear to be may not really be who we are at all. Are you an actor? I don't mean the Shakespearean kind, on the stage, but someone who covers up or hides his or her true feelings, or tries to be everything everyone else wants them to be. This kind of acting is tantamount to lying. How can anyone see your light if you hide it, and deceive them into believing you're someone you're not? To be your true self, you must let people see who you really are inside, how you feel, and what you think. Magic doesn't happen until it is revealed to the audience.

To exude love you've got to stop holding other people responsible for your life and what you've become.

Don't forget that all the folks who have ever done you harm are your teachers, sent to you from the Divine to help you live out this life scenario that you intended in the first place, so why are you so determined to blame the teacher for the student's mistake. In a word: forgive. You know how to do that.

Try, with every fiber of your being, to see the positive in every situation and don't dwell on the negative for too long.

The more time you spend feeling sorry for yourself, the less positive your life will seem. Create an illusion of joy instead. I'm not trying to tell you to fool yourself into thinking that life is a hunky-dory game, but rather create hope in what appears to be a hopeless situation. For example, if you total your car, see it as an opportunity to become a better driver, or to pay more attention to the world around you. Be grateful that you aren't lying in a hospital bed, or even better, that you now have the chance to buy a new vehicle because you have insurance coverage. If you are fired from your job, don't take that as proof that you are useless. See it as an opportunity for spiritual growth. It was time for you to go. God is telling you that a better job is waiting for you, but you were just too stubborn, or probably afraid, to pick up on the signs that were being sent to you from the Universe, and quit that job yourself before you got the boot (sometimes God gets a little heavy-handed, but only because we send the message that we want to learn our lessons that way!). You create the magic in the circumstance. You. You. You.

Love, love, love (the verb).

You've got to give love to get it. If you don't have enough of it in your life, think about how much of it you're handing out. Probably not much. The more you give . . .

Live in Light, Love, and Peace . . .

My church members know this phrase only too well. I have included it as the closing affirmation at every Sunday service. There is an interesting story surrounding it. When I first met my spirit guide, Roger, at the end of our initial, shocking session he told me that I had lots of work to do, and to not be afraid, and know that I was being guided by God. "Now calm down," he said, "Go in Light, Love, and Peace." I loved it so much that it became my personal motto. If we could all just simply go in light, love, and peace, we'd live a life of tranquillity and contentment, and yes, magic.

Just how does one live this ideal? "Living in Light" means living with the unshakable belief that God is the driving force in your life and in the Universe. It means you *trust*. "Living in Love" means that you *believe* that goodness is humanity's basic trait, and that honoring the goodness in everyone honors God. "Living in Peace" means that you *surrender* your tough times, your aggravating moments, your worries, anxieties, pains, and stress to a Higher Power to work through them in a perfect way in your life. Basically, living in Light, Love, and Peace means that you learn to trust, believe, and surrender, to the God that is within you, to help you create a lifetime of happiness.

Does that sound good? It should. It is your birthright. It is what God/Spirit wants for you. So what are you waiting for? Some further instruction? Here it is:

Living in Light, Love, and Peace means:

- Putting God first.

- Listening to your intuition for spiritual guidance.

- Calling upon God to co-create your life.

- Making choices based on how they will affect not only your greater good, but that of all the others involved in any given situation.

- Keeping the above point as your primary goal in dealing with relationships.

- Seeking love out, and giving out tons of it.

- Discovering your life purpose or why you came to the planet.

- Practicing forgiveness for yourself and others.

- Holding no one responsible but yourself for your life and the situations that occur in it.

- Knowing, without a doubt, that you have constant help from God whenever you express the need and ask for it (and even when you don't).

- Remembering to always "trust, believe, and surrender."

Just "Be"

I met a man on a cruise once. He was an interesting soul. He seemed very devoted to his spiritual journey and talked about how he practiced his beliefs and the efforts he made to live a positive and loving life. One evening he was sharing his philosophy of life with me. He said that in his perception, people try too hard to be happy and successful, and that we should all simply take it easy and ". . . just be."

I looked at him as though he was out of his ever-loving mind and said, "Just be? That's it?"

"Yep," he replied. Nothing else.

Being a type-A person and driver personality myself, this concept was foreign to me. "You mean do nothing? Just let life happen, and go with the changes and pursue your dreams without worry or expectation?" I asked.

"Yep," was his response.

Hmmm, I thought. Very interesting.

So, the next day when reflecting upon our talk and his simple, yet powerful remark, I realized that this concept of "just being" was not really revolutionary, it's just that we, myself included, tend to get so wrapped up in the happenings of our daily routine that we forget that idea. This "just be" philosophy translates, in my mind, to peace. Even if my shipmate didn't know himself what he meant, he wasn't going to worry about it. He seemed to have no doubts or fears about how he or his words would be perceived. In his simple way, he was just "being."

Love is like that. It just is. It just happens and we either flow with it or we resist it. We might not be able to put our finger on what love means, exactly, but we definitely know when we're in it. We also know there are all sorts of degrees and types of love, and a myriad of definitions for it. One thing I have learned over time is that love doesn't lend itself to one explanation or another. It's meaning is very subjective. If you were to ask ten people what love means to them, you might get ten very different answers. One thing is for sure, when love is alive within us, we know it. We might not be able to explain it, but we certainly feel and respond to it.

I had been taught in my Catholic upbringing that God is love. God is the ultimate expression of peace, joy, security, and unconditional caring. In my equation, God just is, so if God is love, then love just *is*. That's it. If we can accept that love is a constant in our universe, do we really need to seek further explanation? It seems obvious to me, that since God is within each of us, and God is love, than we are love. We can actually just *be* love. We don't have to do it, or think a lot about it, because it is a part of the core of our very essence. So, when we put it in our heads that we will choose to express God in this lifetime, care for others as we would ourselves, and each day vow to bring joy, compassion, and wisdom to all we undertake, we are *being* love. This is living with purpose. That purpose is demonstrated as you live out each day on this planet.

Crazy Little Thing Called Love

We're used to the flowery kind of human romantic love that gushes from us and makes our hearts pound faster. But when this infatuation ebbs, what is left? If our romantic love is sincere and given freely from the depths of our soul, what is left is what I call true love. This is the feeling that tells us we are safe and secure and totally cared for even when we're not at our best, or when we screw up. That's the way God loves us—truly and uncon- ditionally. If you are committed to living life as a loving person, your difficult times are few and your joyful times many. If you are not committed to being a loving person the opposite is true. You get to control just how much love you'll give, and, consequently, just how much you will receive.

Let's take another look at romantic love. At first a rela- tionship with a lover seems wonderful and flawless, but over time this illusion fades when the day-to-day efforts of life push you to your limits. It is then that you'll know who really loves you. Maybe your relationship is slowly eroding over the years, and is not as good as it used to be. You need to ask yourself if you are both living with joy, compassion, and wisdom, or has doubt, fear, and self-pre-occupation taken over. It is really easy to see if you exude love by the kinds of relationships that you have with others. Who are the people that choose to be with you? Whom do you choose to be with? Do you admire the people in your life, or make excuses for them? It is really simple: love attracts love. If you are not attracting love than you are not exuding it, which simply means that you need to make some changes.

Again, you are probably thinking, "What do I do to express the true love that is the very essence of my being?" Congratulations. Very well put. Here's my formula:

1. Always put God first in your life.

2. See the good (God) in everyone.

3. Be brave; face each day with courage, and enjoy the unfolding of your destiny.

4. Expect the best from the Universe and vow to receive it, and accept it.

5. Contact your divine self daily through prayer and meditation.

6. Don't allow your ego to make your decisions. Use your heart and intuition instead.

7. Provide nurturing, support, and care to those in need, and help others when the opportunity arises.

8. Face life's challenges knowing that you are divinely supported.

9. Have a loving and sincere heart.

10. Just be.

The Opposite of Love Is Fear

Yes, it is true that the opposite of love is not hate, but rather fear. That's probably a new one for you. On your spiritual journey this is one concept you need to remember, especially when you are having difficulty finding the God in someone. Both of these are such strong emotions that psychiatric clinicians say that the human brain cannot compute or process both of them at once. To my untrained mind, that means that if fear is clouding up my gray matter then I am psychologically unable to feel love at that moment. I've thought about this and realized that if I need to sacrifice an emotion, I would rather it be fear than love. How about you? Fear is a very real villain, in that it robs us of the pleasure of people, intimate relationships, and the ability to express God in the world. Any spiritual journeyman needs to get rid of it, pronto!

We have talked about fear before, but the fear I'm talking about now is even more sinister. It is the fear of love itself. Some of us are actually afraid of this, the most basic of emotions. We fear we don't know how to love, or that we're unlovable, or that love carries too much responsibility—therefore we avoid it at all cost. This is a sad situation, particularly for the spiritual seeker, because if one's ability to love is hindered, it follows that one cannot express it. If that is so, then that is the foreshadowing of an unhappy life. It is up to you to decide how you feel about love, in order to know if pursuing the spiritual life is really for you. In this next reflection, I will help you to do that, and release any lingering fear of love you might have, to clear the way to your joy.

Reflection 9

Learning to Love

This exercise is not for the weak of heart. It is meant to get you thinking about how you interpret and express love. I decided that I shouldn't assume that all of us have even felt loved, and that if any readers were learning the difficult lesson of how to recognize and give love, a reflection to clear any blocks and open the heart was in order, to enable love to flow freely through your life. If after performing it you are still uncertain as to what love truly is, the best gift you can give yourself is the affirmation at the end of the chapter. Say it, pray it, until you know it has become true for you, no matter how long it may take. Sooner or later you will break through your self-imposed barriers to love and experience unexplainable joy.

As with the other reflections, assume your comfortable sitting position.

Now, once again, close your eyes, take three gentle breaths, and relax, allowing the relaxation to move from the top of your head, all the way down to the tips of your toes. Reflect upon the following:

As you breathe gently, relax and allow all thoughts to slowly subside from your mind. As you focus on your breathing, tell yourself that you are now open and ready to receive wisdom from the Universe and to open your heart to love. Take this moment and just accept unconditional love from God. Ask Spirit to help you release your fears concerning love, and gently send them away. Then, pause, take a gentle breath, and be at peace.

Now, allow your mind to reflect upon how you feel about the people closest to you. Pick one or two people with whom you are closest and most intimate. Think about your feelings for them. Do you regard them with highest esteem? Would you do anything for them if they were in need? If they did something with which you did not agree, would you abandon the relationship? Are you willing to compromise your own desires to be with them? Are they willing to do the same for you? Are they the kind of people whom you can trust will always act in your best and highest good, and would you, in theirs? Would you say that you "love" them, and that you feel that they "love" you? How would you feel if they were to suddenly be gone from your life? Do you see God in their eyes each time they are with you?

Be honest with yourself and register your answers to these questions in your mind. When you feel satisfied with your responses, take a deep breath, and while exhaling, return to full consciousness, and slowly open your eyes.

Record any interesting information in your journal now. Again, as before, try to write down as many details as you can, as well as your emotional responses.

The Rapture

This being love is a tall order, but you are up to it, or you would not be reading this book! By this step, I'm sure you have come to realize that all the work you have done up to this point will not do you any good unless you choose to love from the depths of your soul. Loving unconditionally is the way God loves us, and is the way we are meant to love ourselves and all other life on the Earth and beyond. Loving means we accept ourselves, others, and our world without judgment or expectation of personal gain. That's the truest form of the emotion, and an incredibly spiritual act. It is also one of the sacred reasons why Spirit has given us the gift of coming to Earth to go through and create this magical life.

So many of us are sadly unsure of just what love is. We think we know, but unfortunately there are too many among us who have not felt loved, and consequently have no clue as to how to express it. An old friend of mine once said that he had no idea what unconditional love was. I was astounded. He had always been kind and loving to me, so I just assumed that he was clear on the emotion. In a very painful conversation, he told me that he had always thought there were conditions to love, and that if we as people screw up, we risk losing it altogether. He said that he had been trying to learn about love all of his life, and the truly sad part of the story is that he was so loved by so many people, but never allowed himself to accept it. I tell you this story not to depress you, but to motivate you, if you are like my friend, to open your heart and show Spirit that you are willing to learn how to give and receive love, which is the most important emotion we will ever experience. If you are willing to do that, you can create a life of magic beyond your wildest dreams. Without it, magic doesn't exist.

And know that as long as God exists, you are loved.

Affirm the following with enthusiasm, and repeat until you *believe* it:

Affirmation 9

"Love is the very essence of my being. I now remove all blocks to my
understanding of Divine Love, and I
receive it, accept it, and give of it
willingly as the one true expression
of my Spirit. And so it is!"

Every morning I have the great pleasure of walking from my bedroom into my office, and beholding a most astoundingly beautiful sight. I live on a bluff overlooking the majestic Hudson River. Through two sets of floor-to-ceiling windows, I can see this incredible body of water and witness not only its beauty, but its ever-changing currents. To top off this experience, as if it were not enough, right out my windows is a small bridge connecting the New York side of the Hudson to the New Jersey side. This bridge is in itself, a work of art. In its supports there are openings that appear to look like angels, wings fully expanded, constantly protecting all who cross. The locals have dubbed it "the Angel Bridge." At night the sight is even more mystical. The contrast of the darkness of the river to the lights of the bridge creates a mirror effect so lovely that it sometimes makes my heart skip a beat. I have my altar set up directly in front of this vista so that I can give thanks to God each day for how very fortunate I am, and how truly blessed.

Step 10

Give Thanks

Be eternally grateful

When one lives in an environment such as this it's easy to be grateful, but the unfortunate fact is that most of us don't have such an "in-your-face" opportunity to be reminded of God's greatness. How then do we begin to feel this emotion? More importantly, when we do feel it, how do we sustain it? In this step, the last, I make a humble attempt at explaining my definition of gratitude, and lead you through the ways in which you can recognize it, sustain this feeling throughout your life, and express it to God, to those you love, and to yourself.

You might already realize that gratitude is a difficult emotion to own, because it requires a decision. Making a decision implies that we assume responsibility, and you know how we humans hate that! To be truly grateful, we must decide to see life from a different perspective. That means that for some of us, we have to change our entire way of thinking and consequently, the way we live.

It took years for me to make the transition from unhappy to grateful. I haven't always lived in a beautiful home overlooking the Hudson. Since this is the last chapter of the book, I thought I might use my own life to illustrate that I, too, had to learn all the lessons and steps I've included in this text. This book is the direct process of my own spiritual journey. I began with the steps I have outlined for you, and now am at a point in my life that is more fulfilling and happy than I have ever known. Finding my Spirit has made all the difference, and it will for you, too, but being grateful is the most powerful key to this kind of fulfillment. If you get nothing else from this book, please get that!

I Got My Lumps!

I have had to take a lot of lumps along the way on my own spiritual path, and I am all the better for it. When I started, I was a struggling actress and director in the theater, with no money and a huge debt. Some days it seemed as though life couldn't get worse. Besides the lack of money, I had to deal with the constant reality that show business is full of rejection. So there you are, totally rejected by life, penniless, jobless, and hopeless. You blame God a lot when you feel like that. You tell yourself that you are just a victim, and you beg God to lighten up on you. "Please, cut me some slack, God," I used to pray. "Why are you doing this to me?" I had no clue at the time, that I was doing "it" to myself. Blame and despair were my constant attitudes. I'm surprised that I had any friends. Who wants to hear about your problems all the time? Friends want to have fun, too. Nonetheless, even though I was blessed with loving, supportive friends, I still didn't feel that I had anything to be grateful for. Then, something terrible happened.

I was working as a director on an off-Broadway play. It was the dream of a lifetime—my dream. Each day when I went to the theater, I couldn't believe that I was actually living out my heart's desire. I had visions of greatness. The next step was Broadway! Wow! Years of studying, rehearsing, starving, hoping, and praying were finally paying off. I was walking on air, so entranced by it all that I was blind to what was actually happening right under my nose. To make a long story short, within a matter of weeks, my life-long dreams were dashed, and I was totally unable to do anything about it. I was fired. The producer was not happy with my work, and rather than telling me what she wanted, she decided to get rid of me instead. For her, that was a lot easier than being honest. When you are in a career like show business, somewhere in the back of your mind you know that people can and will be ruthless. You just don't know if or when you'll be in their path, but that isn't the worst part of the story.

I had been working on the show with my best friend. She was managing the company, a job she got because I convinced the producer to hire her. When I was let go, instead of fighting for me (or quitting herself), she helped the producer find and hire someone else to finish the job. I have never felt so betrayed in my life. This was my best friend! Here I was, no job, no friend, no money, and worst of all, a shattered dream. My career seemed unimportant, all of a sudden. The only thing I could focus on was how miserable I felt and how terrible it was to be sold out by someone you love. I was in really bad shape. Of course, I kept asking God, "Why did you do this to me?" There seemed to be no answer.

Since I was out of work, I sat alone in my apartment grieving, too sad and embarrassed to talk to anyone. One morning I decided to visit my folks in upstate New York. That's when it happened—the gratitude. It took a major cosmic slap in the head for me to realize that I had the unconditional love and support of two of the most wonderful souls on the planet. With that kind of blessed energy ready to cradle and comfort me, no matter what, I suddenly realized how very grateful I was. When my parents hugged me and welcomed me home, it dawned on me that this kind of love was the only thing that mattered in life, because it was God. I had been given the greatest gift anyone could receive. I felt overwhelmingly in awe of how spectacular this gift was and how unappreciative I had been of it for so many years. That moment changed my life forever.

Weeks later, when had I healed my emotional wounds under the care of my incredible parents, I went home to my apartment and decided to change everything about my life. I was so thankful for the opportunity to learn this lesson, I forgave my friend (and myself) and became grateful for what she taught me about myself. I decided to be happy and to appreciate what good I already had in my life, rather than looking for more. Suddenly, everything I owned looked better to me, my friends became closer to me during this trauma, and I realized that there was a reason for this awful experience. At the time, I didn't know what that was, but now I do. If it had not been for that event, I would not have left the theater, moved to upstate New York, founded my church and center, and then written my first book. You, my dear reader, are part of my karma. It is because of you that I have worked through my difficulties to arrive at this point in my life. We are all connected to each other's greatness. For that, we should be eternally grateful.

So, you see, it could take a grand disappointment to make us grateful, but I would recommend the less traumatic route. That's why I have written this chapter. If I can save you the pain, I have given the gift of love that I so abundantly received right back to you. Here follows a much more gentle method of developing an attitude of gratitude, and an appreciation of the blessings of Spirit.

Climbing the Magic Mountain

If you are ready to undertake your spiritual journey, you are ready to climb mountains. It is not an easy path, but it is the most fulfilling, and will help you create an enchanted life. Know that when you open your heart to God through thankfulness, your hike up the magic mountain gets easier. I know that's hard to believe, but it is true. When we are grateful for what we already have in our lives, we begin to see the wonder and delight in the world and all of its beauty. If we can stop worrying and fretting about unimportant day-to-day chores and obligations, and truly appreciate what is important in our lives, struggle subsides. Life doesn't seem so tough. People respond differently to us. As a result of our new awareness of the joys of life and our appreciation of them, we stop expecting so much from ourselves, others, and the world, and learn to enjoy the moment. Frankly, we could get hit by a bus tomorrow and it would be all over, so why waste this day hoping for more, or something better? What you already have is wonderful, if you will just pay attention to it all.

Gratitude Transforms Us

Another benefit of being eternally grateful is that it makes us humble. Our egomania subsides and we're not so proud or vain anymore. We see ourselves as equal to everyone else, just traveling along different paths with different lessons to learn. Gratitude propels us forward on our sacred path and transforms us because it opens up a direct path to God. Each morning as I sit in front of my altar, I thank God for everything that is already mine and all that is yet to be. I know God is listening, because gratitude is like a telephone hot line to Spirit. Offering thanks to the Universe is like picking up your phone and saying, "Hello, God. I'm ready to receive your blessings, so bring them on, bring them on!" I like to fantasize that God would answer, "Get ready, 'cause here I come!" Receiving God's blessings is cause for celebration. There can be no sadness where there is joy. Being grateful teaches us to celebrate and "dance to the music," to steal a phrase.

And Then, God Responds

God responds directly to gratitude. In return for our thankfulness, God gives us more reasons to be grateful. We attract love, riches, health, abundance, and happiness. Our soul expands and exudes positive energy. We become calm about life, and we handle disappointments better. Other people don't hurt us as much, and when things go wrong, we know we can turn back to our Creator for comfort and peace, in our appreciation of what is already in our life. Satisfaction and contentment become real in our world. Even the bad seems not so serious, and the good appears exceptionally wondrous. When we are satisfied and content, we want for nothing, so everything we get is gravy. It is phenomenal that when we stop wishing, hoping, and yearning for things, they fall into our lap. You know this to be true. Once you relax with life, flow happens, doors open, and life runs more smoothly. When life runs smoothly and our body, mind, and spirit are in sync, our consciousness expands. When our consciousness expands, more good energy is released into the Universe, and whatever good we send out comes right back to us, tenfold. You see, gratitude gets you more of what you want, and then some. All you have to do is become aware. Wake up! Then that magic mountain is no sweat to climb.

Giving Thanks

As promised, here are the less traumatic ways in which you can open your heart to the direct path to your greatest good: God.

- Stop denying the good that you already have in your life.

- Don't look at your job, life, or relationships as chores, but see them as a tools for expanding your spirit.

- Think about the people closest to you, how much you love them, and how much they love you.

- If you have pets, allow yourself to soak in the totally unconditional love that they give you so willingly and generously.

- Start seeing the signs of love in other people's eyes.

- Don't compare your life to anyone else's.

- Look forward to the future and be hopeful.

- Take pride in the things you do.

- Be kind to and less critical of yourself.

- Be kind to and less critical of others.

- If you catch yourself gossiping or speaking in negative terms, stop midsentence, and change the subject.

- Do something each day to remind yourself of just how blessed your life is now, today. (Whenever I forget, I just look out my windows!)

- Tell God every day that you are thankful for the gift of life and all the lessons you are learning, and say it until you mean it!

When you do even one or two of the above activities, you will begin to see change happening in the way you perceive life. Then good things slowly begin to materialize in your world. Your magical thoughts of appreciation and gratitude will be the catalyst, working with and within the Universe to change your life and keep you on your spiritual path. Gratitude creates an environment of joy and promise for the future, replacing those feelings of fear, grief, loneliness, despair, and hopelessness. Not bad for just a minimal amount of effort! None of it will happen without your consent, so decide that from this moment on you will be eternally grateful and express it to God frequently and from the bottom of your heart. Then, guess what? Magic happens!

Reflection 10

Thanks, God!

It's time we get personal with God. By now you should know that He/She is listening to all of us, and making direct contact with each one of us. When we open the sacred door to our heart and soul through meditation and prayer, we become aware of this communication. The following reflection will help you to remove any blocks you might have to appreciating your gifts, and it will help you unlock that door to your greatest good. All that you desire can and will be yours when you accept once and for all that God loves you more than anyone, and that Spirit is the Source of all the good in your life. As you do this reflection, keep that thought in mind!

As with the other reflections, assume your comfortable sitting position.

Now, once again, close your eyes, take three gentle breaths, and relax, allowing the relaxation to move from the top of your head, all the way down to the tips of your toes. Reflect upon the following:

As you breathe gently, relax and allow all thoughts to slowly subside from your mind. As you focus on your breathing, tell yourself that you are now open and ready to remove any blocks to your understanding, and are willing to become aware of all the good that already exists in your life, all that you have and possess. For a moment, allow yourself to feel the emotion of gratitude deeply and think about how truly thankful you are for the people you love. Think about all of the things you love about them. Take a few moments to reflect upon how they express their love to you. Feel grateful to God for their presence in your life.

Now shift your consciousness to your body. Allow your thoughts to focus on this wonderful machine and how well it serves you, and thank your body for enabling you to live out this lifetime. If your body is in pain, be thankful for the lesson that the pain is teaching you, and then release it, and be pain free.

Shifting your consciousness once again, allow yourself to fully feel thanks for your mind, and the wonderful gift of thought and reason. Remember how good it feels to figure out solutions to problems, or help someone else through theirs. Feel that joy, and be grateful.

Finally, shift your consciousness to your spiritual self by being grateful for this moment of direct contact with the God within you. Call upon Spirit to be with you always, to help remind you that you are a magnificent being, an energy that has chosen to live out this human lifetime, to learn, grow, and express God on Earth. Vow to stay connected to your Creator, through your gratitude for this life and all that comes along with it. In this moment, thank God for helping you open your being to unconditional love. Feel it, accept it, and be thankful for it, even if it moves you to tears, and allow this Divine Energy to be part of your consciousness, always.

Now, take a deep breath, and while exhaling, return to full consciousness and slowly open your eyes.

Record any interesting information in your journal now. Again, as before, try to write down as many details as you can, as well as your emotional responses.

You should be very excited for yourself after completing this reflection. If you were unaware of the impact of God in your life, my advice now is to wait and watch for the signs of joy and fulfillment you have just invited into your world. When you meditate upon gratitude you are expressing it. This expression acts like a chain reaction in the Universe and you send waves of Light that return to you as love, peace, joy, and abundance.

The Magic Show

It's time for the finale to your magic show. Time to pull the rabbit out of the hat, and take a chance that will pay off big for you, if you can go the distance. You have made a commitment to yourself to grow in consciousness, awareness, and love. It has taken courage to admit that you might need some help along the way, and that you might not have been sure of your motive for moving along this path in life, but you know it is right for you and that it feels like who you are or whom you want to become. There is no greater gift that you can give yourself than the opportunity to welcome your highest and greatest good into your life. Committing to and following a spiritual path is a holy and profound undertaking that will lead to a life that has great meaning and is fulfilled in every way. I salute you and encourage you to create the life you want, and make magic happen each day. Fight on, my friends, because the spoils of war for the spiritual warrior are the sacred awareness of Divine Presence constantly working in and through you, and the blessing of a life lived beyond your wildest dreams—beyond belief.

Affirm the following with enthusiasm, and repeat until you *believe* it:

Affirmation 10

"I am eternally grateful and thank
God for everything that is already
mine, and all that is yet to come. Today, I create a magical life filled with
love, joy, health, prosperity, and abundance, far beyond my imaginings. I
gratefully accept this wonderful life
and vow to remain in direct contact
with the Divine within me, living always in the state of grace, and walking with Spirit in Light, Love, and
Peace. And so it is!"

May God bless you!
Go in Light, Love, and Peace.
And so it is!

Conclusion

I hope you enjoyed the book and are ready to create a magical life and commit to your personal spiritual journey with enthusiasm and joy. I would love to hear from you as you pursue your divine path. Write me in care of Llewellyn, at the address stated in the "To Write to the Author" section at the beginning of this book.

You may also request a list of my audiocassette lectures on positive spiritual living.

You can also write to me online, or request information about my books and audiocassette lectures on positive spiritual living, at

www.AdrianCalabrese.com.

For information about the Metaphysical Center and the Metaphysical Church of the Spirit, visit

www.TheMetaphysicalCenter.org.

Thanks for reading, and may God bless you on your journey!

Glossary

Affirmations—Positive statements that inform God of what we want to draw into or eliminate from our lives. When carefully worded and spoken, an affirmation works on an unseen level to focus our spiritual energy and can help us to change the course of our lives.

Angel—One of the most powerful loving energies in the Universe, assigned by God to protect and guide humans and all other forms of life. They are sacred energies that have never had a physical lifetime. Angels are the guardians of all life, and even guide us through and beyond our death.

Block—A negative thought, fear, or doubt that mentally stops us from achieving our goals in life. Blocks occur within our subconscious mind, and may be known or unknown to our conscious mind. One's spiritual journey should begin by eliminating all blocks, including doubt and fear, from the consciousness of the seeker.

Divine Plan—The set of lessons we choose to learn, or our predesigned plan for our current lifetime. We form the Divine Plan along with God while we are in spirit form, before we are born or reincarnate. We decide for ourselves who we will be, what lessons we will learn, and how we will learn them. It is our destiny.

Divine Will—A combination of what God wants for us, and what we want for ourselves. Our will and the Divine Will are one and the same, because God exists within us.

Energy—A powerful source of invisible, usable power that exists in all things, animate and inanimate.

Enlightenment—The goal of the spiritual seeker, enlightenment is the state in which we achieve direct communion with God. Our consciousness has expanded to the point that we no longer need to reincarnate to learn lessons, but rather, we can return to the Earth as a master teacher such as Jesus, or the Buddha, if we so choose.

Free Will—Our God-given right to make any choice we wish, take any path we desire, and be whomever we want to be.

God/Spirit/Universe/God-Mind—The Source of all creation—life itself. The one-mind and perfect intelligence from which everything in the Universe was created. God is the beginning and the end, the all-good, all-loving energy that pervades the cosmos. It is an immanent, neutral Spirit energy that loves and supports Its creations. All life comes from It, and returns to It.

Higher Consciousness—Also known as our Higher Self, Spiritual Self, or Intuitive Self, it is the part of us that is beyond our physical body, the God within, in direct contact with all the energies of the Universe. Our Higher Consciousness is our Spirit, our Soul. It is best to rely on this force within us, since its prompting is always correct, very powerful, and guides us to our greater good.

Intuition—It is also known as the Psychic Self. This is the part of the human mind that is open to the unseen energies of the universe. Through it we can receive thoughts, impressions, pictures, and sounds from other planes of existence, and send strong messages to the Universe, through positive intention and mental imaging.

Karma—Also known as the Universal Law of Cause and Effect, we create positive or negative karma through our thoughts, words, and actions, and the way in which we live our life. Karma can bridge lifetimes, and when unresolved, can follow us through the ages and affect our future lives. Basically, karma means that the energy of whatever we do, think, or say comes back to us in some form. How we resolve or deal with it determines the positive or negative events, relationships, and happenings in our lifetime.

Lessons—All of the events of our lives, both good and bad, designed to help us learn to grow spiritually. We may move on spiritually only when a lesson is learned. Lessons will repeat themselves, or negative events of our lives will grow in intensity until we have realized, understood, and learned that lesson. Then our soul will learn new lessons, enabling us to reach our highest spiritual clarity or potential—enlightenment, or oneness with God.

Life Purpose—The reason for reincarnating in this lifetime. The overall life purpose of humans is to serve God and each other, and how we choose to do that is up to us. We each have a distinct life purpose based upon our karma, talents, wants, and needs of this lifetime. The life purpose is individualized by our choices, or the specific way in which we decide to serve God and man.

Manifesting—The ability to draw, attract, and make real in physical form our thoughts, wishes and desires. Also known as "demonstrating."

Meditation—A silent form of introspection, prayer, and relaxation. One assumes a comfortable sitting position, generally closes the eyes and allows all thoughts to leave the mind, while concentrating on a peaceful idea or image, hence achieving an altered state of consciousness.

Metaphysics—The mystical study of the existence of all life energy within the Universe, both physical and beyond, and its relationship to God. This is a positive philosophy that recognizes man's unique nature embodying a mind, body, and Spirit, working together as a single unit, yet connected to all life, helping man create a loving, abundant, peaceful existence in service to God, others, the Earth, and all its life-forms.

Psychic Ability—This is the capacity to discern information from deeper levels of the mind or consciousness, and other planes of existence. The person with a highly developed psychic sense can receive and send powerful messages in thought form.

Reflection—A form of meditation that gently guides one to think about and reflect upon one's life and spiritual goals, in order to better understand how to change, adjust, or maintain one's thoughts and perceptions, to create the life one wishes to live, simply and peacefully.

Reincarnation—A belief that the soul can pass from one body to another after death, and live a new lifetime. Previous lifetimes are known as past lives. Information from these past lives can shed light on the karma and lessons carried over that have yet to be resolved in the current lifetime.

Ritual—A personal or public spiritual practice, performed with regularity, to worship, give thanks, or manifest, by recognizing and honoring the existence of a Higher Power, and Its assistance in our lives.

Spirit Guide—An energy entity existing within the scope of the unseen universe, whose function is to advise, guide, and assist humans in living a positive, abundant, and peaceful life. Spirit guides are energies that have lived in human form, and have an agreement with a specific individual, made prior to reincarnation, to remain as a helper in spirit, while the individual lives out a physical lifetime. Guides, as they are known, are our best friends in spirit, helping us get through the day-to-day struggles of life.

Spirituality—The state of being that is beyond all religious dogma. A way of thinking and living life in flow with the Power that created us. A spiritual person chooses to live an aware existence committed to the growth of his or her soul toward oneness with God, always mindful of his or her thoughts, words, and actions, and the effect they have upon his or her own life, others, and the world.

Spiritual Journey—The lifelong path of a spiritual person toward his or her spiritual goals and eventually enlightenment or oneness with God. Our journey may begin at any age and will enable us to live a life of joy, prosperity, love, and peace.

Synchronicity—A term coined by Carl Jung to describe the meaningful coincidences that occur in our lives. The term implies that the Universe is not random, and that all things happen for a reason. Therefore, there really are no coincidences, only meaningful synchronicities, happening just as they are meant to happen, in perfect order, and in their perfect time.

Universal Laws—Spiritual principles by which our soul is governed on the mental plane of thought. They are invariable, constant, and regular, and apply to everyone, believer or not. If the seeker chooses to understand, accept, and follow these laws as he or she lives his or her spiritual journey, their life will be in flow with the God-Force and all struggle, pain, fear, and doubt will be easily released from their life.

Visualization—Visualization is a form of mental imaging, in which the mind forms pictures of its own creation. The images formed are powerful thoughts that can be used to manifest, to help individuals achieve a personal best, find spiritual peace and direction, and to heal the body of disease.

Bibliography

Addington, Jack and Cornelia. *Your Needs Met*. Marina del Rey, Calif.: DeVorss & Company, 1986.

Belhayes, Iris, with Enid. *Spirit Guides: We Are Not Alone*. San Diego, Calif.: ACS Publications, Inc. 1985.

Daniel, Alma, Timothy Wylie, and Andrew Ramer. *Ask Your Angels*. New York: Ballantine Books, 1992.

Levoy, Gregg. *Callings: Finding and Following An Authentic Life*. New York: Three Rivers Press, 1997.

Ming-Dao, Deng. *365 Dao: Daily Meditations*. San Francisco, Calif.: Harper San Francisco, 1992.

Ponder, Catherine. *Open Your Mind To Receive*. Marina del Rey, Calif.: DeVorss & Company, 1987.

_____. *The Dynamic Laws of Prayer*. Marina del Rey, Calif.: DeVorss & Company, 1987.

_____. *The Dynamic Laws of Prosperity*. Marina del Rey, Calif.: DeVorss & Company, 1985.

Robertson, Jane L., and Deborah Hughes. *Metaphysical Primer: A Guide To Understanding Metaphysics*. Boulder, Col.: Metagnosis, 1991.

Roman, Sanaya. *Spiritual Growth: Being Your Higher Self*. Tiburon, Calif.: H. J. Kramer, Inc., 1989.

Sherwood, Keith. *Chakra Therapy: For Personal Growth and Healing*. St. Paul, Minn.: Llewellyn Publications, 1993.

Smith, Huston. *The World's Religions*. San Francisco, Calif.: Harper San Francisco, 1991.

Sutphen, Dick. *Finding Your Answers Within*. New York: Pocket Books, 1989.

Taylor, Terry Lynn, and Mary Beth Crain. *Angel Wisdom: 365 Meditations and Insights from the Heavens.* San Francisco, Calif.: Harper San Francisco, 1994.

Wilde, Stuart. *Infinite Self: 33 Steps To Reclaiming Your Inner Power.* Carlsbad, Calif.: Hay House, Inc., 1996.

Williamson, Marianne. *Illuminated Prayers.* New York: Simon & Schuster, 1997.

Yogananda, Paramahansa. *Metaphysical Meditations.* Los Angeles, Calif.: Self-Realization Fellowship, 1994.

Index

☾ REACH FOR THE MOON

Llewellyn publishes hundreds of books on your favorite subjects! To get these exciting books, including the ones on the following pages, check your local bookstore or order them directly from Llewellyn.

Order by Phone
- Call toll-free within the U.S. and Canada, 1-877-NEW-WRLD
- In Minnesota, call (651) 291-1970
- We accept VISA, MasterCard, and American Express

Order by Mail
- Send the full price of your order (MN residents add 7% sales tax) in U.S. funds, plus postage & handling to:
  Llewellyn Worldwide
  P.O. Box 64383, Dept. 0-7387-0311-7
  St. Paul, MN 55164-0383, U.S.A.

Postage & Handling
- **Standard** (U.S., Mexico, & Canada)

If your order is:
  $20 or under, add $5
  $20.01–$100, add $6
  Over $100, shipping is free

(Continental U.S. orders ship UPS. AK, HI, PR, & P.O. Boxes ship USPS 1st class. Mex. & Can. ship PMB.)

- **Second Day Air** (Continental U.S. only): $10 for one book plus $1 per each additional book
- **Express** (AK, HI, & PR only) [Not available for P.O. Box delivery. For street address delivery only.]: $15 for one book plus $1 per each additional book
- **International Surface Mail:** $20 or under, add $5 plus $1 per item; $20.01 and over, add $6 plus $1 per item
- **International Airmail:** Books—Add the retail price of each item; Non-book items—Add $5 per item

Please allow 4–6 weeks for delivery on all orders.
Postage and handling rates subject to change.

Discounts
We offer a 20% discount to group leaders or agents. You must order a minimum of 5 copies of the same book to get our special quantity price.

Free Catalog
Get a free copy of our color catalog, *New Worlds of Mind and Spirit*. Subscribe for just $10.00 in the United States and Canada ($30.00 overseas, airmail). Call 1-877-NEW-WRLD today!

Visit our website at www.llewellyn.com for more information.

Includes 6 easy steps to Success

Adrian Calabrese, Ph.D.

How to Get Everything You Ever Wanted

Complete Guide to Using Your
Psychic Common Sense

How to Get Everything You Ever Wanted

Adrian Calabrese, Ph.D.

When Adrian Calabrese's faithful car bit the dust, she was broke and had already maxed out seven credit cards. She went looking for her dream car anyway, and by the end of the day she was the proud owner of a shiny Jeep Cherokee. It was all because she had found the secret formula for getting what she wanted. Not long after that, money began flowing in her direction, and she paid off all her debts and her life turned around. Now she shares her powerful method of applying ancient concepts of inner wisdom to everyday life. Starting today, anyone can begin immediately to get everything out of life he or she desires.

With this book you can follow the sure-fire six-step method for drawing whatever you want into your life; give yourself a psychic tune-up; discover your hidden talents, creativity, and artistic abilities, and use them to give your manifesting work a final blast of energy. Use any of the sixty affirmations to help you manifest your specific goals. Learn ways to ensure that your request to the universe has been transmitted, and call upon the loving energies of angels and spirit guides to give extra power to your requests

1-56718-119-8, 7½ x 9⅛, 288 pp.   **$14.95**

Write Your Own Magic:
The Hidden Power in Your Words

Richard Webster

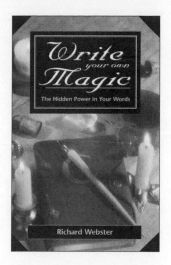

Write your innermost dreams and watch them come true! This book will show you how to use the incredible power of words to create the life that you have always dreamed about. We all have desires, hopes and wishes. Sadly, many people think theirs are unrealistic or unattainable. *Write Your Own Magic* shows you how to harness these thoughts by putting them to paper.

Once a dream is captured in writing it becomes a goal, and your subconscious mind will find ways to make it happen. From getting a date for Saturday night to discovering your purpose in life, you can achieve your goals, both small and large. You will also learn how to speed up the entire process by making a ceremony out of telling the universe what it is you want. With the simple instructions in this book, you can send your energies out into the world and magnetize all that is happiness, success, and fulfillment to you.

0-7387-0001-0, 5³⁄₁₆ x 8, 312 pp.   **$9.95**

The Lost Secrets of Prayer: Practices for Self-Awakening

Guy Finley

Do your prayers go unanswered? Or when they are answered, do the results bring you only temporary relief or happiness? If so, you may be surprised to learn that there are actually two kinds of prayer, and the kind that most of us practice is actually the least effective.

Best-selling author Guy Finley presents *The Lost Secrets of Prayer,* a guide to the second kind of prayer. The purpose of true prayer, as revealed in the powerful insights that make up this book, is not to appeal for what you think you want. Rather, it is to bring you to the point where you are no longer blocked from seeing that everything you need is already here. When you begin praying in this new way, you will discover a higher awareness of your present self. Use these age-old yet forgotten practices for self-awakening and your life will never be the same.

When you open *The Lost Secrets of Prayer* you will discover: seven silent prayers that will turn your life around; the purpose of true prayer; how to touch the timeless truth; the secret power in practicing ceaseless prayer; how to make all of life be just for you; how to get more from the universe than you ask for; the real danger of wasted energies; how to develop the unconquerable self in you; and 125 special insights to aid your personal inner work

1-56718-276-3, 5¼ x 8, 240 pp. **$9.95**

The Karma Manual:
9 Days to Change Your Life

Dr. Jonn Mumford
(Swami Anandakapila Saraswati)

Many Westerners talk about karma, but few really know much about it. Now Dr. Jonn Mumford provides a clear, practical guide, featuring the traditional yet innovative approach of his first guru, Dr. Swami Gitananda Giti of India.

Karma is a simple law of consequence, not of moralistic retribution and penalty. It's a way of viewing existence that results in increased mental health and self-responsibility.

Discover the different types of karma. Process your personal karma by clearing out unwanted automatic actions—thus lessening the amount and rate at which new karma accumulates. Finally, learn a very direct method for "deep frying" the karmic seeds in your being through the Nine-Day Karma Clearing Program.

1-56718-490-1, 5³⁄₁₆ x 8, 216 pp.   **$9.95**

TO ORDER, CALL 1-877-NEW-WRLD
Prices subject to change without notice

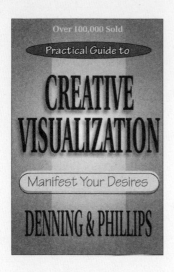

Practical Guide to Creative Visualization:
For the Fulfillment of Your Desires

Denning & Phillips

All things you want must have their start in your mind. The average person uses very little of the full creative power that is potentially his or hers. It's like the power locked in the atom—it's all there, but you have to learn to release it and apply it constructively.

If you can see it . . . in your mind's eye . . . you will have it! It's true: you can have whatever you want, but there are "laws" to mental creation that must be followed. The power of the mind is not limited to, nor limited by, the material world. *Creative Visualization* enables humans to reach beyond, into the invisible world of astral and spiritual forces.

Some people apply this innate power without actually knowing what they are doing, and achieve great success and happiness; most people, however, use this same power, again unknowingly, incorrectly, and experience bad luck, failure, or, at best, an unfulfilled life.

This book changes that. Through an easy series of step-by-step, progressive exercises, your mind is applied to bring desire into realization! Wealth, power, success, happiness, even psychic powers . . . even what we call magickal power and spiritual attainment . . . all can be yours. You can easily develop this completely natural power, and correctly apply it, for your immediate and practical benefit.

0-87542-183-0, 5³⁄₁₆ x 8, 264 pp.   **$9.95**

Perfect Timing:
Mastering Time Perception
for
Personal Excellence

Von Braschler

How would you like to run faster, think more quickly, and project yourself instantly wherever you want to go? This book will show you the secrets of athletes who "freeze" time to accomplish amazing feats, and of investors who seize opportunities at the perfect moment. You will witness ordinary people enter heightened states of awareness that saved their lives. And you will learn how to control time.

Perfect Timing incorporates scientific evidence that time is elastic and subject to our will and intent. In the realm where the limitations of physical laws do not apply, anyone can learn to astral project, heal at a distance, practice remote viewing, bi-locate, meditate, and reach higher consciousness.

0-7387-0212-9, 6 x 9, 212 pp.   **$14.95**

TO ORDER, CALL 1-877-NEW-WRLD
Prices subject to change without notice